THE MANDATE: DISCIPLESHIP

Salvation Is Just the Beginning!

DR. RICK BARKER

Bibliography:

Watchman Nee – Spiritual Authority – Copyright 1972 Christian Fellowship Publishers, INC. New York ISBN 0-935008-35-7

Robert Coleman, The Master Plan of Evangelism, 1963, 1964, 1993, Revel a division of Baker Publishing Group, Grand Rapids, MI ISBN 978-0-8007-8808-7

Why tongues? By Kenneth E. Hagin , 31 p . © Kenneth E. Hagin Evangelistic Association, Inc.; 15 Aug75; A661938. A66 1967 Brother Kenneth E. Hagin, "The Holy Spirit and His Gifts"

Strong's concordance Author: W. E Vine, James Strong ISBN:9780785242543, 0785242546 Published:1999 Publisher: T. Nelson Publishers

Ken Walker quotes Herb Miller from his book "How to Build a Magnetic Church" Published 1987

Matthew Henry Commentary Originally written in 1706, Matthew Henry's six volume Complete Commentary provides an exhaustive look at every verse in the Bible.

New Testament in Modern Speech ISBN:1575620251; ISBN13:9781575620251 Release Date: July 2012 Published by Harrison House Inc (2012)

THE MESSAGE: The Bible in Contemporary Language
Copyright © 2002 by Eugene H. Peterson. All rights reserved.
THE MESSAGE Numbered Edition copyright © 2005

Scripture taken from the Amplified Bible (AMPCE), Copyright © 1954, 1958, 1962, 1964, 1965, 1987 by The Lockman Foundation. Used by permission.

Scripture taken from the New King James Version®. Copyright © 1982 by Thomas Nelson. Used by permission. All rights reserved.

Scripture quotations marked (NIV) are taken from the Holy Bible, New International Version®, NIV®. Copyright © 1973, 1978, 1984, 2011 by Biblica, Inc.™ Used by permission of Zondervan. All rights reserved worldwide. www.zondervan.com The "NIV" and "New International Version" are trademarks registered in the United States Patent and Trademark Office by Biblica, Inc.™

Scripture quotations marked (TLB) are taken from The Living Bible copyright © 1971. Used by permission of Tyndale House Publishers, a Division of Tyndale House Ministries, Carol Stream, Illinois 60188. All rights reserved.

ACKNOWLEDGEMENTS

There are so many who have encouraged me in the ministry over the last nearly 30 years. I have been blessed to have some of the greatest mentors and generals of the faith pour into my life.

I want to thank my pastor, Dr. Mark T. Barclay, for believing in me, ordaining me, and bringing me into the Righteous Preachers Network in 2008. His standard of holiness and excellence have inspired me immensely all these years. Amy and I are richly blessed to have both him and his lovely wife, Mrs. Vicki Barclay, in our lives.

I also want to thank Jason Gatlin for the amazing cover design and Pastor Chris McMichael and his team at Petra Publishing. What a powerful blessing and resource they are to so many.

To my amazing warrior of a wife, Amy--you have been a champion of my life and ministry from the moment we met. I am so grateful that God blessed me to have you as my wife. I love you and am looking forward to many years of life and ministry together as we pursue God's assignment in these last of the last days!

TABLE OF CONTENTS

FOREWORD

I've been preaching this gospel since the 1970s. I have always been concerned about the many people who are born again but never become a true disciple. And we all know that just because one is born again doesn't mean they're fixed yet, nor does it mean they have the ability to turn their life totally over to Christ.

I am proud of this book, The Mandate. It is going to help many believers walk more closely with Christ, be overcomers, and live a life free from their shackles and bondages. It is also going to equip leaders in our great Kingdom to help make disciples who are even more committed and live with biblical precision. Every pastor's dream is to build a great army who will never betray God and stay together until the trumpet sounds.

This book will provide the means by which to do this. The information we need is on these pages from Dr. Rick Barker who is not only a longtime disciple but also a man who has pastored God's people.

I love how Rick used the stories of real Bible characters to drive home this point: "This is not a new problem." The eight points made in Chapter 2, "The Heart of the Father," are worth purchasing the entire book.

This is one of those books you'll want to read through more than one time, looking up the verses and letting them settle within your heart. Then, either buy your friends a copy, or pass yours on so it continues to bring perpetual impartation to the body of Christ.

This book is easy to understand, written by a man who has walked down this path—both on the side of the pastorate and as a disciple. It's a great study guide and loaded with verses. Job well done, Rick. May the Lord breathe on the sale and distribution of this, and may it be used to build one of the greatest armies Jesus Christ has ever had—those of us who are going to help climax the ages!

— Mark T. Barclay
PREACHER OF RIGHTEOUSNESS

INTRODUCTION

The goal of this book is to provide a tool in the hand of ministers and ministries that will allow them to equip and release people to a new level of doing the work of the ministry. Today, an alarming number of pastors are leaving the ministry, and churches are closing their doors at a rate exceeding those being planted. Let's start our time with looking at the number of pastors leaving the ministry.

A recent study released in 2021 states that roughly 1% of the nation's pastors leave the ministry every year for reasons other than death or retirement. While that may not sound like a lot in real numbers it is number now over 4500 per year versus 20 years ago when there were 1500 per year. Of the number that leave here are the reasons given:

- Conflict with the church
- The church is not a good fit
- Family issues, 13% moral issues
- Personal burnout
- Personal finances
- Illness

Now to church closures. Changes in public policy and public expectation following the 2020 COVID-19 shut down have had a devastating effect on the church. Many de-emphasized the gathering together of the church as being important. According to Religious News Service (www.religionnews.com) at the completion of a decade-long study ending in 2020, between 3,780 to 7,700 churches closed annually compared to approximately 3,000 opening on average in 2019, that number declined from 4,000 in 2014.

What is the answer? According to God's design and plan, those who are called to be in the fivefold ministry must fulfill Ephesians 4:12, "to equip the saints for the work of the ministry for the edifying of the Body of Christ." If the saints are not equipped for the work of the ministry, then evangelism is stagnant and non-existent. At best, the growth that we experience is usually "transfer growth" from other ministries with people who are running to hide from leadership's attempts to bring growth and correction to their lives. Another reason for this kind of growth may be that some are spiritually malnourished believers who have not been getting the teaching needed to become what God has called them to become.

Additionally, the saints must allow themselves to be equipped to make disciples. When disciple-making is lacking, it affects all areas of the ministry. The lost are not won, new disciples are not made and the ministry of helps suffers. The domino effect then proceeds to put pressure on the pastor, the staff, and the few who choose to faithfully serve.

There is a mandate placed on the body of Christ that must be fulfilled! What is a mandate? By definition, a mandate is an official order or commission to do something. The last words of Jesus were meant to have weight and impact on the Body of Christ. Jesus said in Matthew 28:18-20 (NIV):

> *"All authority in heaven and on earth has been given to me. Therefore, go and make disciples of all nations, baptizing them in the name of the Father and of the Son and of the Holy Spirit, and teaching them to obey everything I have commanded you. And surely I am with you always, to the very end of the age."*

I grew up in a church where much of what was being done, the senior pastor was doing. He would mow the lawn, fix the plumbing, and keep the buses and vans mechanically sound. He would visit the sick, the new converts and the new families, and counsel those in crisis. As the years went by, I began to participate as a preteen and so did some others. The result of continually loading the pastor with all the responsibilities of the body meant he did not have the opportunity to give himself continually to prayer and the ministry of the Word. The result was disastrous because as he and the congregation aged, more and more families left for "greener pastures" where they thought they could be fed. I do not endorse leaving a church for just any reason-- you must follow God's leading in regard to leaving a church. If you are not being equipped, many times you do not feel you have any other option.

I left that church for two reasons. First, I was not where I needed to be spiritually. The pastor, I am sure overwhelmed by the load of the church, was trying his best to keep everything going. Second, I left after the pastor and I had a disagreement regarding my desire to step away from a ministry that I felt ill-equipped to serve in. I was a Sunday school teacher but I was not living a life that reflected the integrity of someone teaching others. When I approached him about stepping down his response to me was not the greatest, but, I should have handled it differently. About two years after I left this church, I went back to this pastor and repented for leaving.

The pastor was a wonderful man who loved God. I got to spend some time with him and his wife years later. I discovered that they were never really taught how to carry a congregation beyond an initial commitment to Christ. I took this opportunity to learn from this aged man of God. Solomon gives an illustration in the book of Proverbs that I'd like to refer to.

> *I went by the field of the lazy man, and by the vineyard of the man devoid of understanding; And there it was, all overgrown with thorns; Its surface was covered with nettles; Its stonewall was broken down. When I saw it, I considered it well; I looked on it and received instruction: A little sleep, a little slumber, A little folding of the hands to rest; So, shall your poverty come like a prowler, And your need like an armed man. (Proverbs 24:30-34 NKJV)*

We must take the time to look around, not in judgment, but to observe the ministries that have had struggles. If you can glean anything from the voice of wisdom of the ministers who led those ministries, it will save you a tremendous amount of trouble.

A great point of wisdom I gleaned from this senior minister was to continually pursue growth, training, and education. I also learned that the relationships of those in authority over me and those whom I call friend are just as important as pursuing training in the ministry. These work hand-in-hand with one another! Proverbs 27:17 says, "As iron sharpens iron". You want relationships with people who are looking out for your improvement. The equipping of the congregation is very important however as ministers of the gospel, we must be sure the relationships we have and the authority in our lives are equipping us and taking us higher.

THIS IS NOT A NEW PROBLEM

The problem of people wearing out in the ministry is not something new. We can see in scripture that after the children of Israel left Egypt, they were about to wear Moses out. After leading them out of Egypt, Moses was trying to handle everything. We see in Exodus 18, that Moses' father-in-law came and heard all that God had done for the children of Israel and he rejoiced. But he visited, he observed how Moses sat, from morning till evening, and judged the issues among the people.

So Moses' father-in-law said to him, "The thing that you do is not good. Both you and these people who are with you will surely wear yourselves out. For this thing is too much for you; you are not able to perform it by yourself. Listen now to my voice; I will give you counsel, and God will be with you: Stand before God for the people, so that you may bring the difficulties to God. And you shall teach them the statutes and the laws, and show them the way in which they must walk and the work they must do. Moreover, you shall select from all the people able men, such as fear God, men of truth, hating covetousness; and place such over them to be rulers of thousands, rulers of hundreds, rulers of fifties, and rulers of tens. And let them judge the people at all times. Then it will be that every great matter they shall bring to you, but every small matter they themselves shall judge. So it will be easier for you, for they will bear the burden with you. If you do this thing, and God so commands you, then you will be able to endure, and all this people will also go to their place in peace." (Exodus 18:17-23 NKJV)

Moses gave heed to this instruction; and as a result he was more able to bear the load. There were rulers over thousands, hundreds, fifties and tens, but it still was not quite enough. We can see in Numbers 11, Moses gets a bit overwhelmed by the people, and we see him whining to God, as many of us have done.

Then Moses heard the people weeping throughout their families, everyone at the door of his tent; and the anger of the Lord was greatly aroused; Moses also was displeased. So Moses said to the Lord, "Why have You afflicted Your servant? And why have I not found favor in Your sight, that You have laid the burden of all these people on me? Did I conceive all these people? Did I beget them, that You should say to me, 'Carry them in your bosom, as a guardian carries a nursing child,' to the land which You swore to their fathers? Where am I to get meat to give to all these people? For they weep all over me, saying, 'Give us meat, that we may eat.' I am not able to bear all these people alone, because the burden is too heavy for me. If You treat me like this, please kill me here and now—if I have found favor in Your sight—and do not let me see my wretchedness!" So the Lord said to Moses: "Gather to Me seventy men of the elders of Israel, whom you know to be the elders of the people and officers over them; bring them to the tabernacle of meeting, that they may stand there with you. Then I will come down and talk with you there. I will take of the Spirit that is upon you and will put the same upon them; and they shall bear the burden of the people with you, that you may not bear it yourself alone. (Numbers 11:10-17 NKJV)

In verse 13, Moses reveals that he has really lost focus on the fact that God has already taken care of them when he says, "Where am I to get meat to give to all these people?" Then in verse 15, he wants God to kill him; broken focus will make us do and say some very foolish things. But we can be thankful that we serve a God who looks beyond our frailties and who remembers we are dust. So, God steps in to bring order to the leadership of the nation. The rulers over the thousands, fifties, hundreds, and tens are now looking to the seventy for their instruction, correction, and accountability.

God, from the beginning, never intended for a lone man to do it all. If man could do it all alone then he would not have to totally rely on God. This cannot be so, "for without faith it is impossible to please God," (Hebrews 11:6). Another problem that can occur when one man tries to "do it all" is the "super martyr" mentality. God steps in when we think we are the only ones and shows us by His still, small voice that He has reserved for Himself those who will faithfully do His work.

We see in the New Testament that the same issue of the work being too much caused a problem for the Body of Christ. In Acts 6, as the number of the disciples grew and multiplied, widows were neglected and it caused conflict. The twelve apostles called everyone together and declared that it was not good for them to leave the Word of God and serve tables. Now please understand this, I am not saying anyone is above serving tables. The Apostles only said that it was not good for them to leave the Word of God and serve tables. We can see that the wisdom of God prevailed and the answer was found.

"Therefore, brethren, seek out from among you seven men of good reputation, full of the Holy Spirit and wisdom, whom we may appoint over this business; but we will give ourselves continually to prayer and to the ministry of the word." And the saying pleased the whole multitude. And they chose Stephen, a man full of faith and the Holy Spirit, and Philip, Prochorus, Nicanor, Timon, Parmenas, and Nicolas, a proselyte from Antioch, whom they set before the apostles; and when they had prayed, they laid hands on them. Then

the word of God spread, and the number of the disciples
multiplied greatly in Jerusalem, and a great many of the
priests were obedient to the faith. (Acts 6:3-7 NKJV).

Notice that the Apostles did not do the choosing, but they gave that task to the congregation so they could continue to dedicate themselves to prayer and the ministry of the Word.

Here, we see the beginning of the ministry of helps in the New Testament here and the result was wonderful. Acts 6:7 says that the Word of God spread and the number of the disciples multiplied greatly. The scriptures show that the work so touched the lives of people that a great many priests were obedient to the faith. Our obedience to make sure that no one person has to do it all is imperative to the continued growth of the Kingdom of God.

Over the years, I have watched both full-time pastors and lay leaders alike wear themselves out trying to do everything. Though God never intended it to be that way, I have been guilty of myself and a few times it resulted in physical problems. Today, however, I have realized through the Word of God that it is not desirable that I leave prayer and the ministry of the Word to wait tables when I should be equipping those of good reputation, full of the Holy Spirit and wisdom who may be set over the work of taking care of the widows, cleaning the church, doing hospital visitation, doing youth ministry, ushering; and… the list goes on.

Again, this does not mean I do not do any of those things, but the worst thing for a man of God to do is try to do it all and never afford or give the people the opportunity to serve. We are never excused from being with people in times of need and crisis but we must allow God to use us to raise up others for the work of the ministry, so the effectiveness of the Gospel is not hindered.

As we continue in this study, we must start by looking at the current state of the Body of Christ and its effectiveness in reaching and retaining those who need Jesus. I believe that we are in a time when a great shift is taking place, and we must run with endurance the race that is set before us so that we may hear the words of Jesus in Matthew 25:21, "well done, good and faithful servant." As we continue my prayer for the Body of Christ comes from the Apostle Paul in the letter to the church at Ephesus.

> *Therefore I also, after I heard of your faith in the Lord Jesus and your love for all the saints, do not cease to give thanks for you, making mention of you in my prayers: that the God of our Lord Jesus Christ, the Father of glory, may give to you the spirit of wisdom and revelation in the knowledge of Him, the eyes of your understanding being enlightened; that you may know what is the hope of His calling, what are the riches of the glory of His inheritance in the saints, and what is the exceeding greatness of His power toward us who believe, according to the working of His mighty power. (Ephesians 1:15-20 NKJV)*

May the Lord give you understanding and wisdom as we grow and conform to the image of His Son and we expand upon the Word concerning our effectiveness in the ministry.

GOD'S PURSUIT OF MAN

I want to take a journey through the scriptures and see that from the very beginning God has pursued man to walk in close relationship with Him. As we continue, let us glean the principles that He laid down for us to walk in to see the results that He has received through time. When we look from the beginning, God made everything good! There is nothing He created that was not good.

> Then God said, "Let Us make man in Our image, according to Our likeness; let them have dominion over the fish of the sea, over the birds of the air, and over the cattle, over all the earth and over every creeping thing that creeps on the earth." (Genesis 1:26 NKJV)

God gave man full dominion over the earth and all that was in it, but the dominion was not all God was looking for. God was looking to walk in the closest of intimacy with man. He gave Adam a command to tend and keep the garden; he could partake of every tree of the garden but there was one tree that he was to tend only. God forbade Adam to partake of the tree of knowledge of good and evil.

> *Then the Lord God took the man and put him in the Garden of Eden to tend and keep it. And the Lord God commanded the man, saying, "Of every tree of the garden you may freely eat; but of the tree of the knowledge of good and evil you shall not eat, for in the day that you eat of it you shall surely die." (Genesis 2:15-17 NKJV)*

It was after this that God made the helper for Adam who was called alongside.

> *And the Lord God caused a deep sleep to fall on Adam, and he slept; and He took one of his ribs, and closed up the flesh in its place. Then the rib which the Lord God had taken from man He made into a woman, and He brought her to the man. And Adam said: "This is now bone of my bones and flesh of my flesh; She shall be called Woman, because she was taken out of Man." (Genesis 2:21-23 NKJV)*

Now Adam is not just responsible as steward of the garden but he also carries the responsibility to lead his wife. Matthew Henry says that God being her father, did not leave Eve to her own disposal but brought her to Adam. She was not allowed to make her own choice of whether or not to marry or who to marry but was under the divine direction of God her Father.

> *Evidence of the purity and innocence of that state wherein our first parents were created, v. 25. They were both naked. They needed no clothes for defense against cold nor heat, for neither could be injurious to them. They needed none for ornament. Solomon in all his glory was not arrayed*

like one of these. Nay, they needed none for decency; they were naked, and had no reason to be ashamed. They knew not what shame was, so the Chaldee reads it. Blushing is now the color of virtue, but it was not then the color of innocence. Those that had no sin in their conscience might well have no shame in their faces, though they had no clothes to their backs. (Henry, Genesis 2:21-25 KJV)

Prior to this, point they did not know good or evil but all they knew was found in God alone. In Genesis 3, the story turns tragic in that man took upon himself something that did not belong to him. He ate of the fruit of the tree of the knowledge of good and evil, and it cost him the place of intimacy with God. So began a journey that caused God to implement the plan of the redemption of fallen man in order to have that place of intimacy He once had.

Watchman Nee is one of my favorite authors on the subject of authority. He brings a point to illustration that I am speaking of here in that our actions should not be governed by the knowledge of good and evil, but by our obedience to God.

By taking the fruit of the tree of the knowledge of good and evil, they found a source of right and wrong in other than God Himself. Consequently, after the fall, men need not find in God the sense of right and wrong. They have it in themselves. This is the result of the fall. The work of redemption is to bring us back to place that we will now find right and wrong in God. (Nee, P21)

I plan to illustrate through this book the course that God took through the Old Testament record in His pursuit of man. Over and over and over again man has gotten off course, but God has been faithful in His pursuit to make sure the plan of redemption has been and will continue to be carried out through all time on this earth. Let's look now at some of the biblical examples of God's pursuit of man.

NOAH

In Genesis 6, we see that mankind had grown and multiplied on the earth and God said "My Spirit shall not strive with man forever." (Genesis 6:3) But the evil on the earth was getting greater, and greater and God became sorry that He had created man.

> *Then the Lord saw that the wickedness of man was great in the earth, and that every intent of the thoughts of his heart was only evil continually. And the Lord was sorry that He had made man on the earth, and He was grieved in His heart. So the Lord said, "I will destroy man whom I have created from the face of the earth, both man and beast, creeping thing and birds of the air, for I am sorry that I have made them." But Noah found grace in the eyes of the Lord. (Genesis 6:5-8 NKJV)*

Noah found grace in the eyes of the Lord. The Hebrew word used for grace here is chên meaning graciousness, that is, subjectively (kindness, favor) or objectively (beauty): —favour, grace (-ious), pleasant, precious, [well-] favored. Noah was found to be one in God's sight who had His favor. Evidently, Noah had not allowed the thoughts and pursuits of his heart to become evil. But finding favor with God, Noah was given the very important assignment of preserving the human race as well as every beast and animal on the earth. The task was huge and building an ark was just the beginning. Can you imagine the detail that God gave Noah? It is believed that the earth had never had rain but was watered by a mist; mankind had never seen a catastrophic event in all of time. When Noah began to build imagine what temptation he had to resist so he would not give up but fulfill the assignment given by God. This assignment had with it the incentive that God would make a covenant with Noah, and that the race of man would be preserved, and the line of redemption would run through his lineage.

But I will establish My covenant with you; and you shall go into the ark—you, your sons, your wife, and your sons' wives with you. (Genesis 6:18 NKJV)

All that was really required of Noah was obedience to God in building the ark. For 120 years he faithfully, day in and out, built the ark declaring, "there's a flood coming." Let us not forget that Noah was not a young man, for the Word declares that in the six hundredth year of Noah's life when he boarded the ark and was shut in while the rain came upon the earth. There he waited for seven days before the waters of the deep gushed up and the rains came down. If Noah had gotten impatient and left the ark, he would have ruined the plan. But thanks be to God for the patience and obedience of Noah and his family to stay in the ark. They could not allow themselves to be moved by what they saw or heard. They had to follow in complete obedience in faith to God. For forty days and nights it rained on the earth, purging the earth of the evil upon it. Everyone who did not listen to Noah perished in the flood of judgment upon the evil earth.

And all flesh died that moved on the earth: birds and cattle and beasts and every creeping thing that creeps on the earth, and every man. All in whose nostrils was the breath of the spirit of life, all that was on the dry land, died. So, He destroyed all living things which were on the face of the ground: both man and cattle, creeping thing and bird of the air. They were destroyed from the earth. Only Noah and those who were with him in the ark remained alive. And the waters prevailed on the earth one hundred and fifty days. (Genesis 7:21-24 NKJV)

Then as we see in Genesis 8, the Word tells us that God remembered Noah. God is mindful of us and is looking out for the things that concern us. God could not leave Noah in the ark because there had to be a time of release to repopulate the earth. For approximately one year, Noah and his family inhabited the ark, but now it was time to leave the ark and fill the earth.

Go out of the ark, you and your wife, and your sons and your sons' wives with you. Bring out with you every living thing of all flesh that is with you: birds and cattle and every creeping thing that creeps on the earth, so that they may abound on the earth, and be fruitful and multiply on the earth. (Genesis 8:16-17 NKJV)

God gave the command of increase upon the earth. It was not a suggestion; it was a command. Upon leaving the ark, Noah made an altar upon which to sacrifice to God a burnt offering. He understood covenant, that without the shedding of blood there is no remission of sin.

As the smoke arose, it came to the nostrils of God and was well pleasing to Him. So pleasing was this sacrifice that God swears to never again curse the earth or destroy it as He had (Genesis 8:21 NKJV).

In Genesis 9, God once again gave Noah the command to be fruitful and multiply and fill the earth, as well as adding the revelation that he had dominion over the animals: "the fear of you and the dread will be on every beast of the earth" (Genesis 9:2 NKJV). As God established covenant with man through Noah and his family, He gave a sign of that covenant by placing the rainbow in the cloud that He would remember the everlasting covenant with man to never again destroy all flesh as He had done.

ABRAHAM

As we begin to look at Abraham's life, let's begin just before God called him to leave all and go to a land He would show him. We see that after Noah and the flood, man continued to move back to the place where the pursuits of his heart were evil. He tried to make his own way to God in building the tower of Babel.

Everything they did was centered around self; they did not pursue God to see what His plan was.

As God looked down on their pursuits, He saw that nothing would be impossible for them. The problem was not in making advancements in the earth but the fact that God was nowhere to be found in their plans. So, God confused their language and scattered them throughout, the earth so that there would not continue to be a pursuit of the things that would allow man to move toward self-sufficiency. If they had continued on the track they were on, they would have possibly ruined the redemption for all mankind.

But God who sees the end from the beginning called Abram a man who God would separate and establish for Himself a race and people through which His plan of redemption could be carried out.

Get out of your country, from your family and from your father's house, to a land that I will show you. I will make you a great nation; I will bless you and make your name great; and you shall be a blessing. I will bless those who bless you, And I will curse him who curses you; and in you all the families of the earth shall be blessed (Genesis 12:1-3 NKJV).

To execute Gods full plan, Abram had to separate himself from his family since their business was idol-making. God set forth the plan, making the prize so much greater than the price. Take note of the faith that Abram had to walk in--he did not have written scripture to refer to but had to walk in a personal revelation of the living God of all creation.

Being seventy-five years old at this point Abram forsook all, that is all (except Lot, his nephew) and leaves his country. As we look further, having Lot and his family created a problem for the herdsmen of Abram and Lot. Strife developed, and they had to separate anyway (Genesis 13). Just a note, what we compromise to keep we will ultimately lose, and we risk causing great harm if we do not fully obey the instruction of God.

Lot ends up choosing Sodom, much to his own detriment, for as he settled there, the depravity of the land becomes quite clear. To top it all off, in the midst of everything, Lot is taken captive in a war of rebellion with Chedorlaomer, whom they had served for twelve years. In the end, Abram has to go and rescue Lot. Often, when we chose our own way, we end up crying out to God for deliverance because of the choice we made.

To save lot Abram takes servants, pursued and attacked the kings and their areas. Abram rescues Lot and gets back the goods the King of Sodom had lost. Abrams met Melchizedek and gave him a tithe of all. Melchizedek then brings out bread and wine, the sign of covenant and blesses Abram (Genesis 14). The king was so overwhelmed that he tells Abram to keep the goods and give him the people. But Abram did not give in to the temptation of a shortcut, but he looks to God for his blessing:

> Now the king of Sodom said to Abram, "Give me the persons, and take the goods for yourself." But Abram said to the king of Sodom, "I have raised my hand to the Lord, God Most High, the Possessor of heaven and earth, that I will take nothing, from a thread to a sandal strap, and that I will not take anything that is yours, lest you should say, 'I have made Abram rich'—except only what the young men have eaten, and the portion of the men who went with me: Aner, Eshcol, and Mamre; let them take their portion. (Genesis 14:21-24 NKJV)

Abram proved himself trustworthy to God. Every action of our lives will either prove our faithfulness or will prove to God that we cannot be trusted. In making this declaration Abram drew another step closer to God in a covenant relationship with Him. It was after this that God came to him declaring that He is Abram's protection. But Abram looks for proof that this is so asking, "What will you give me, seeing I go childless" (Genesis 15:2).

Now you could look at these two ways: Abram got his eyes on the circumstance or he began to understand that covenant is a two-way street. I believe from the response here that he is realizing that in a relationship there is responsibility on each party in order for the benefits to truly be realized. God surely would have corrected Abram if this were an issue of only getting his eyes on circumstance. But what happens here is the promise of God that the servant born in his house would not be his heir, but one who was to be born of his loins.

As God continues to speak, we come once again to that place of sacrifice where Abram is instructed to bring an offering to God. Once again, without the shedding of blood there is no remission of sins. (Hebrews 9:22 NKJV)

So, He said to him, "Bring Me a three-year-old heifer, a three-year-old female goat, a three-year-old ram, a turtledove, and a young pigeon." Then he brought all these to Him and cut them in two, down the middle, and placed each piece opposite the other; but he did not cut the birds in two. And when the vultures came down on the carcasses, Abram drove them away. Now when the sun was going down, a deep sleep fell upon Abram; and behold, horror and great darkness fell upon him. Then He said to Abram: "Know certainly that your descendants will be strangers in a land that is not theirs, and will serve them, and they will afflict them four hundred years. And also, the nation whom they serve I will judge; afterward they shall come out with great possessions. Now as for you, you shall go to your fathers in peace; you shall be buried at a good old age. But in the fourth generation they shall return here, for the iniquity of the Amorites is not yet complete." And it came to pass, when the sun went down and it was dark, that behold, there appeared a smoking oven and a burning torch that passed between those pieces. On the same day the Lord made a covenant with Abram, saying: "To your descendants I have given this land, from the river of Egypt to the great river, the River Euphrates— the Kenites, the Kenezzites, the Kadmonites, the Hittites, the Perizzites, the Rephaim, the Amorites, the Canaanites, the Girgashites, and the Jebusites." (Genesis 15:9-21 NKJV)

God speaks prophetically to Abram about the children of Israel and their future bondage and deliverance by God. Now when God makes a promise, it is up to Him to fulfill it, not us. Yes, we must stay on the side of righteousness but that is the only condition we must fulfill.

Unfortunately, Abram had not yet learned the lesson that God is responsible for fulfilling His promise. As we get to Genesis 16, Sarai comes up with a plan to give Abram an heir. (We cannot make our own way for the plan of God.) The result of this work of the flesh was disastrous and has resulted in the conflict between the children of promise and that which was a work of the flesh through the centuries and will continue until the day that Jesus rules and reigns on the earth.

The result of Abram's blunder was that for 10 years he did not hear from God. When Abram was ninety-nine, God had to basically start all over again. But thank God His mercy endures forever, for God looks to the prize also.

Oh, give thanks to the Lord, for He is good! For His mercy endures forever. (1 Chronicles 16:34 NKJV).

God declares once again that He will make a covenant with

Abram and admonishes him to walk blameless before Him. Now we see a transformation take place in that God changes his name to Abraham and declares, "I have made you a father of many nations." (Genesis 17:5 NKJV). Notice that God placed that promise in the past tense, Romans 4:17 says, God calls those things that be not as though they are and we must be no different. Within that year, Sarai (who is now Sarah) bears a son, the son of promise. The plan of redemption takes another step forward, through the lineage of Abraham, Isaac and Jacob, are born the multitude of the children of Israel through whom the Messiah is born.

JOSEPH

Joseph was born the son of Jacob, being the favored son he was greatly hated by his brothers. But God had destined Joseph for greatness and given him a dream in which his brothers, father and mother bow down to him. Instead of keeping it in his heart he shares it with the family and they hated him even more. Joseph's youth got the best of him and his immaturity cost him his freedom and nearly his life. A lesson that we all would do well to learn and heed here is that of discretion. God made sure the pursuit of His plan of redemption was preserved. But his brother cooked up a different plan.

Jacob sent him out to check on his brothers and make sure all was well. Then seeing him coming they started a plan to kill him. But you know God will even use someone who hates you at times to preserve your life for Reuben delivered him out of their hands. He really was not much better than his brothers for he still allowed them to strip Joseph of his coat and throw him in a pit. Then he said nothing to keep them from selling him to the Ishmaelite traders so Judah speaks up, "what profit is there if we kill our brother?" (Genesis 37:26). He makes the suggestion to sell Joseph and for twenty pieces of silver they sell him out.

Much to the grief of his father, the brothers of Joseph lie to him implying that Joseph is dead as evidenced by his bloody coat that they present to him.

But Joseph was alive and well. He was bought by Potiphar (captain of the guard) who was an officer of Pharaoh. Joseph came into favor with Potiphar as he served him and Joseph was promoted to being overseer of all that was his master's. As always, the devil kept quiet till an opportunity arises. Now, Potiphar's wife attempted to get Joseph to sleep with her. But Joseph looks to the integrity of his relationship with God and tells her, "How can I do this great wickedness and sin against God?" (Genesis 39:9) Day after day she hounded and badgered him until, she got tired of his refusal to accept her advances and decides enough is enough. She attempts to take him by force but Joseph flees the temptation leaving his robe behind in the process. She quickly schemes and makes up a story that he tried to rape her and Potiphar being left with no choice has to either kill Joseph or place him in prison. Knowing his wife like he must have he chose the latter. Even those who did not know God played a role in the preservation and pursuit of God to man. Potiphar, being the captain of the guard was in charge of executions but decided it was better to put Joseph in jail. Your integrity will always deliver you. Joseph being put in prison, did not fret or get into the flesh, he allowed God to move on his behalf. He did not try to make things happen on his own but waited for the deliverance of God.

While in jail Joseph grew in favor and ended up overseeing the jail. One day he interpreted the dreams of the chief butler and baker of Pharaoh. Though forgotten for a time after this, in due season, God delivered him as he is brought into the presence of Pharoah and tells him the interpretation of his dreams. Pharaoh was so impressed with the wisdom of Joseph that he makes him second in command to himself. With the coming famine, Joseph stored up twenty percent each year leading up to the famine in the land so that there would be food in Egypt. The result was that there was also enough to sell to the regions around, and through this Joseph's brothers were sent to Egypt to buy grain. They were not aware they would come face to face with the one whom they had sold into slavery.

> *Then Joseph could not restrain himself before all those who stood by him, and he cried out, "Make everyone go out from me!" So, no one stood with him while Joseph made himself known to his brothers. And he wept aloud, and the Egyptians and the house of Pharaoh heard it. Then Joseph said to his brothers, "I am Joseph; does my father still live?" But his brothers could not answer him, for they were dismayed in his presence. And Joseph said to his brothers, "Please come near to me." So, they came near. Then he said: "I am Joseph your brother, whom you sold into Egypt. But now, do not therefore be grieved or angry with yourselves because you sold me here; for God sent me before you to preserve life. (Genesis 45:1-5 NKJV)*

But, instead of chastising his brothers he helped them understand that though they intended it for evil, God had a plan. Joseph was sent ahead to preserve life. If he had not been in Egypt, would the children of Israel have been preserved through the famine? Thank God we will never have to figure that one out for God made a way despite the ill intended by man and the enemy He preserved the Israelite nation.

MOSES

Moses was used mightily of God, but he first had to come to the end of himself so that it would be God's plan and pursuit of the redemption of mankind and not the plan and pursuit of Moses. From his mother's womb, he was called to be a deliverer. But, just because an assignment is programmed in us does not mean that we should make it happen in our time on our terms.

We pick up the story in Exodus 2, where Moses, having a heart for his people, he sees one of them suffering and beaten at the hand of an Egyptian leader. Moses, in defense of his fellow Israelite, killed the Egyptian. This gets Moses noticed immediately by Pharaoh and he had to flee if he was to live to see another day. Coming to the land of Midian, that spirit of a deliverer came on him again as he defended the priest of Midian's daughters who are trying to water their father's flock and were being run off by the shepherds. This gets the attention of the priest and Moses is content to live with him and marries his daughter Zipporah.

In your call, you really are not ready to be launched out until you are ready to stay where you are. Moses was content and tending the flock of his father-in-law when he was visited by the Angel of the Lord. Moses had to come to the end of himself. Can you imagine if Moses had been allowed to deliver or attempt to deliver the children of Israel prior to this time? It would have been a mess! The conquest would not have been by the supernatural power of God but by the work, zeal, and aggression of man. Can you see the mess that would have been created if Moses had continued in the direction he was going? It's the same with our efforts. When we operate in our zeal or in our own fability then we create a work of the flesh and not a work that is done by the supernatural power of God.

Let's get back now to the visitation of God in the pursuit of man. God appeared to Moses in the burning bush and told Moses exactly who He is and what Moses' assignment was. Let's pick this up in Exodus 3.

> God said, "I've taken a good, long look at the affliction of my people in Egypt. I've heard their cries for deliverance from their slave masters; I know all about their pain. And now I have come down to help them, pry them loose from the grip of Egypt, get them out of that country and bring them to a good land with wide-open spaces, a land lush with milk and

honey, the land of the Canaanite, the Hittite, the Amorite, the Perizzite, the Hivite, and the Jebusite. "The Israelite cry for help has come to me, and I've seen for myself how cruelly they're being treated by the Egyptians. It's time for you to go back: I'm sending you to Pharaoh to bring my people, the People of Israel, out of Egypt." (Exodus 3:7-9 The Message Bible)

God is confident of His plan, purpose and assignment for our lives. We must express our confidence in His plan by our obedience. Without action on our part there is no proof that we really believe Him. Here Moses immediately began to look for reasons why this plan would not work.

First, he looked at himself and said "who am I?" God's answer, "I will be with you!" God even gives him proof and says the sign is that you will worship Me on this mountain. Moses seemed to begin to progress by asking, "who do I tell them sent me?" God said, "I AM" sent me to you. As we look further at Exodus 4, Moses began to look once again for an escape asking, "But what if they will not believe?" So, God performs a miracle through the rod in Moses' hand by turning it to a serpent and then God gave him the sign of leprosy and the water turning to blood.

Was that enough to get Moses to keep moving forward? No! Moses then said, I am not eloquent of speech. Compared to God, I think we would all feel that way. Ultimately, Moses moves forward when God adds Aaron to the team and said you shall be as God to him and he shall speak for you.

Going back to Egypt, they came before Pharaoh, and just as God had told Moses, Pharaoh refuses to let the children of Israel go. We must learn when God has a plan, we must be faithful to complete our assignment so that His glory is revealed.

Through each plague Pharaoh hardened his heart. He was not moved by the water turned to blood, not the frogs, the lice, the flies, the diseased livestock, boils, hail, locust or darkness. God announced the death of the firstborn but even this was not enough for Pharaoh.

Moses instituted the Passover where the blood of a lamb, without spot or blemish, was to be placed on the posts of the doors. This was a sign that the death angel would not touch the firstborn within that house. What broke Pharaoh was the death of his firstborn! Finally, Israel was free to go but they did not go out empty. Instead, they plundered the Egyptians in their going. But God was not finished working supernaturally. Pharaoh pursued Israel and tried to overtake them. However, what was light to Israel was extreme darkness to Egypt and they could not come near Israel. God gives the command as to which way to go so that Israel will see further that God wants to do this supernaturally. He displayed mightily that He is the "I AM". The children of Israel ended up hemmed in between Pharaoh and the Red Sea. Greatly intimidated by this, they thought and began to complain that Moses had set them up.

Then they said to Moses, "Because there were no graves in Egypt, have you taken us away to die in the wilderness? Why have you so dealt with us, to bring us up out of Egypt? Is this not the word that we told you in Egypt, saying, 'Let us alone that we may serve the Egyptians'? For it would have been better for us to serve the Egyptians than that we should die in the wilderness." And Moses said to the people, "Do not be afraid. Stand still, and see the salvation of the Lord, which He will accomplish for you today. For the Egyptians whom you see today, you shall see again no more forever. The Lord will fight for you, and you shall hold your peace." And the Lord said to Moses, "Why do you cry to Me? Tell the children of Israel to go forward. (Exodus 14:11-15 NKJV)

Our responsibility is not to question what we see with our eyes. We should not allow our senses to be in control of life and come between us and obeying God. The reality is that when God gives an instruction to a leader and we complain, our complaint is not against them, it is against God.

We need to arrest ourselves and follow the command of God to "go forward!" I would dare say that if Israel would not have moved on, they would have been consumed by Egypt. But as they went forward, God opened the Red Sea and the children of Israel went through on dry land to the other side and the deliverance God told them would come was done with a great manifestation of the destruction of the enemy.

Then the Egyptians shall know that I am the Lord, when I have gained honor for Myself over Pharaoh, his chariots, and his horsemen." And the Angel of God, who went before the camp of Israel, moved and went behind them; and the pillar of cloud went from before them and stood behind them. So, it came between the camp of the Egyptians and the camp of Israel. Thus, it was a cloud and darkness to the one, and it gave light by night to the other, so that the one did not come near the other all that night. Then Moses stretched out his hand over the sea; and the Lord caused the sea to go back by a strong east wind all that night, and made the sea into dry land, and the waters were divided. So, the children of Israel went into the midst of the sea on the dry ground, and the waters were a wall to them on their right hand and on their left. And the Egyptians pursued and went after them into the midst of the sea, all Pharaoh's horses, his chariots, and his horsemen. Now it came to pass, in the morning watch, that the Lord looked down upon the army of the Egyptians through the pillar of fire and cloud, and He troubled the army of the Egyptians. And He took off their chariot wheels, so that they drove them with difficulty; and the Egyptians said, "Let us flee from the face of Israel, for the Lord fights for them against the Egyptians." Then the Lord said to Moses, "Stretch out your hand over the sea, that the waters may come back upon the Egyptians, on their chariots, and on their horsemen." And Moses stretched out his hand over the sea; and when the morning appeared, the sea returned to its full depth, while the Egyptians were fleeing into it. So, the Lord overthrew the Egyptians in the midst of the sea. Then the waters returned and covered the chariots, the horsemen, and all the army of Pharaoh that came into the sea after them. Not so much as one of them remained. But the children of Israel had walked on dry land in the midst of the sea, and the waters were a wall to them on their right hand and on their left. So, the Lord saved Israel that day out of the hand of the Egyptians, and Israel saw the Egyptians dead on the seashore. Thus, Israel saw the great work which the Lord had done in Egypt; so, the people feared the Lord, and believed the Lord and His servant Moses. (Exodus 4:18-31 NKJV)

God will not be mocked; His plan of redemption could not be thwarted by any purpose of any leader throughout time. Pharaoh chose to stand in the way of God's plan, and it brought about great destruction for Egypt. The plan of God's redemption moved on.

In the wilderness on the way to the promised land, God had to get the children of Israel ready for what they would ultimately possess so the Law is given. To move to the future, they had to unhook from the past of being in a land given to idolatry and gross decadence. God gave Moses the specific plan of worship and how to maintain good standing with God, but even while on the mountain the people get impatient because Moses is gone for so long and they have Aaron create them an idol.

We must never let our past experience form for us the image of God in our lives. If we don't deal with our flesh it will keep us from being transformed into His image. For the Children of

Israel, God had just about had enough, and was ready to destroy them when Moses stepped in and interceded for them.

> *Then Moses pleaded with the Lord his God, and said: "Lord, why does Your wrath burn hot against Your people whom You have brought out of the land of Egypt with great power and with a mighty hand? Why should the Egyptians speak, and say, 'He brought them out to harm them, to kill them in the mountains, and to consume them from the face of the earth'? Turn from Your fierce wrath, and relent from this harm to Your people. Remember Abraham, Isaac, and Israel, Your servants, to whom You swore by Your own self, and said to them, 'I will multiply your descendants as the stars of heaven; and all this land that I have spoken of I give to your descendants, and they shall inherit it forever.'" So, the Lord relented from the harm which He said He would do to His people. (Exodus 32:11-14 NKJV)*

Every godly leader will get on their face before God when people rise up and ask for mercy; remember, you reap what you sow. Looking at what took place, Moses was not only interceding for the people, but he was truly considering what this would do to God's image. I am not saying that God needs a public relations firm to help Him. Maybe it was truly a test of Moses' character to see whether he would stand in the gap and put God in remembrance of His covenant to Abraham, Isaac and Jacob. Therefore, God relented of what He said he would do to Israel. Looking through the book of Leviticus, much work remained: the building of the tabernacle, the articles of the tabernacle of God, the Ark of the Covenant, the implementation of offerings and sacrifices, feasts, and celebrations. All of these had to be completed as they prepared to enter the land God had sworn to give them through Abraham, Isaac, and Israel.

As we get to the book of Numbers, we see they were instructed by God the assignment that each tribe was to carry out. God gave further instruction about the unclean, the laws concerning confession and restitution, the unfaithful wife, the Nazirite, the priestly blessing, offerings of the leaders, the arrangement of the lamps, and the cleansing and dedication of the Levites.

With the second Passover and the command to move from Sinai, the people complained against Moses for not having meat to eat. Moses caved in at this point, crying out to God, "Where am I to get meat? Did I conceive this people?" Really, it seems God ignored Moses' tantrum and goes on to tell him to gather seventy men of the elders of Israel. God never intended one man to carry forward the plan of redemption and the growth and care and equipping of His people alone. Moses got overwhelmed because he started falling into the trap that this was all on his shoulders and not God's. But God was so gracious and anointed those seventy to help.

Then I will come down and talk with you there. I will take of the Spirit that is upon you and will put the same upon them; and they shall bear the burden of the people with you, that you may not bear it yourself alone. (Numbers 11:17 NKJV)

God sent Moses' help by anointing leaders to have the wisdom and insight to lead with Moses' direction. Further, He sent meat to them--so much so that they could not handle it. One last roadblock came when Aaron and Miriam began to complain against Moses because he had married an Ethiopian woman. We must always keep pride in check! God can speak to each one of us as well as our leader. But it is when we think He speaks to us more than to our leaders we will find ourselves in real trouble.

God heard what Aaron and Mariam said about Moses and He was not happy. Remember this no matter what: God knows what you say and do. The question we should ask, "Is He pleased with what we are doing?" Miriam became a leper and Moses once again interceded, but God responded that she would be healed but she must remain outside the camp seven days. Delays are disappointing but a delay does not always mean an aborting of the plan of God.

In Numbers 13, the next instruction came to send spies to the land of Canaan. Each tribe was to sent out a spy. The instruction is clear:

> Then Moses sent them to spy out the land of Canaan, and said to them, "Go up this way into the South, and go up to the mountains, and see what the land is like: whether the people who dwell in it are strong or weak, few or many; whether the land they dwell in is good or bad; whether the cities they inhabit are like camps or strongholds; whether the land is rich or poor; and whether there are forests there or not. Be of good courage. And bring some of the fruit of the land." Now the time was the season of the first ripe grapes. (Numbers 13:17-20 NKJV)

The instruction seemed simple enough, but the problem came when they add their opinion to the report. They let fear influence their thoughts as to whether or not they could defeat the inhabitants of the land. Sometimes, the enemy blinds our minds as to the great things that God has done for us. Look at the report:

> Then they told him, and said: "We went to the land where you sent us. It truly flows with milk and honey, and this is its fruit. Nevertheless, the people who dwell in the land are strong; the cities are fortified and very large; moreover, we saw the descendants of Anak there. The Amalekites dwell in the land of the South; the Hittites, the Jebusites, and the Amorites dwell in the mountains; and the Canaanites dwell by the sea and along the banks of the Jordan". (Numbers 13:27-29 NKJV)

When the report came, rather than remembering the great deliverance that God brought for them, when He opened the Red Sea and they crossed on dry land. They also lost sight of the drowning the army of Egypt, God's provision of manna, meat, water, even their clothes didn't wear out. The very fact that they came out of Egypt with not one feeble among them but they focused on what was before them as though God had done nothing to deliver them in their past. Of the twelve sent out, there were found only two who remembered that God was the One who gave the instruction to possess the land. As a result, they are the only ones who forty years later came in with the strength of their youth and possessed the land as God had promised. Again, though delayed, the plan of God was not denied.

We could go on and on looking through the Old Covenant and see, through great men and women, God pursued man to redeem him. Think of it, Joshua was mentored by Moses and took in the children of Israel to possess the land. Then God raised up Gideon and Ruth, Samuel and David. Though there were obstacles and efforts by the enemy of our souls to try to destroy the plan of redemption, Gods plan and purpose prevailed. Next we will look at the New Covenant, and we will see God prepared the way for Jesus through John.

JOHN THE BAPTIST

After 400 years of prophetic silence, we meet Zacharias a priest of God tending his duties in the temple. Here he is visited by an angel of the Lord who tells him that Elizabeth, his wife, will have a son and he will be named John.

And you will have joy and gladness, and many will rejoice at his birth. For he will be great in the sight of the Lord, and shall drink neither wine nor strong drink. He will also be filled with the Holy Spirit, even from his mother's womb. And he will turn many of the children of Israel to the Lord their God. He will also go before Him in the spirit and power of Elijah, 'to turn the hearts of the fathers to the children,' and the disobedient to the wisdom of the just, to make ready a people prepared for the Lord". (Luke 1:14-17 NKJV)

In disbelief, Zacharias asked, "How will this happen?" and proceeded to argue with the angel. So the angel gave him a sign, and he became mute and unable to speak till John is born. Sometimes we need to just be quiet so we don't ruin the work of God with our tongue. After the birth of John, his tongue was loosed, and he gave glory to God. As John grew, he stepped into the office God had ordained for him. We can see from the prophetic word to his father that John would prepare the way of the Lord. John daily proclaimed only that he was preparing the way and that he is not the One to come.

John answered, saying to all, "I indeed baptize you with water; but One mightier than I is coming, whose sandal strap I am not worthy to loose. He will baptize you with the Holy Spirit and fire. His winnowing fan is in His hand, and He will thoroughly clean out His threshing floor, and gather the wheat into His barn; but the chaff He will burn with unquenchable fire." And with many other exhortations he preached to the people. (Luke 3:16-18 NKJV)

He clearly stated that they should look for someone else. John knew he was nearing the end of his assignment. In Luke 3:21-22, Jesus Himself comes and is baptized to fulfill all righteousness. As He came out of the water the Holy Spirit descends upon Him and God spoke from heaven, "You are my beloved Son, in You I Am well pleased." As Jesus' ministry began, John's ended and his words echoed the heart of a true servant of God, "He must increase, but I must decrease". (John 3:30 NKJV)

God's pursuit of man is evident throughout the passage of time in all that we have seen from Adam to Jesus. God's passion is for people. He does not want anyone to miss the opportunity of spending eternity with Him.

2

THE HEART OF THE FATHER

As we continue our study, let's focus on the foundation of the Father's heart through the study of Jesus' ministry here on earth. I want to get into the meat of what Jesus did in His pursuit of man's redemption from sin, to walk forgiven and empowered for this life and that which is to come.

After His baptism, Jesus overcame the temptation in the wilderness resisting the enemy using God's word declaring, "It is written." As we look through the Gospels, we can see that there was a complete plan that Jesus used to raise up those who would carry on His work after He returned to the Father. In his book, The Master Plan of Evangelism, Robert Coleman lays out the following principles:

1. Selection
2. Association
3. Consecration
4. Impartation
5. Demonstration
6. Delegation
7. Supervision
8. Reproduction

SELECTION

It is evident in Luke 6:13 that although there were many disciples around Jesus who were being developed, He only initially selected twelve whom He called apostles. His strategy was not with massive meetings to make disciples but rather to first train up those who could lead the masses. "Men were to be His method of winning the world to God." (Coleman 27).

To be a true disciple, you must be willing to learn. A disciple is defined as "a learner or pupil under the instruction or influence of another; one who is passionate about the doctrine of the teacher." Following the example of Jesus, we can see that His main focus was on just a few; first with the twelve, then with the seventy. He never neglected the masses but used those settings to teach and instruct in more general terms.

Why didn't Jesus just muster a great massive army at His coming to earth? Why not mobilize and have masses of believers from the start? Because His goal was not to impress anyone but to bring the Kingdom of God and the plan of God to the earth. The plan of God is not in a ministry being personality-driven. God chose to use man starting with the twelve Jesus selected. The twelve were to then lead more people to a genuine relationship with God, rather than a sense-driven, emotionally-moved and charged experience with God.

I am not against mass meetings for evangelistic purposes. However, it is important, that there also are masses of people waiting to personally disciple those who have been won. Usually, mass meetings do not net a large number of people for the long-term. Typically, without proper follow up, less than 10% of those won in a crusade will connect with a local church. The history of man shows that humanity is easy prey for idolatry, and without true leadership from a Shepherd, they will follow almost anything.

The first step to building a team is selecting the right leaders that God can use to guide people. Then, through training and equipping, individuals who can lead and disciple others so that as the numbers added are fruit that remains. If Jesus Himself chose not to lead the masses, what makes us think that we can lead them? He never ordained this approach, look at the Word. I challenge you to find where He took it all upon Himself to lead a large number of people without appointing and anointing others around Him to help train and equip the saints. If the Head of the Church chose others to help him lead, no one human being can be effective in trying to do it all by themselves.

Out of all the disciples that followed Him, He first chose twelve. They spent the next three and a half years being equipped for the work to come. This may have been why the religious leaders of the day could not believe that Jesus was the Messiah. They were looking for someone who lined up with their opinion and imagination of what God had in mind. But they failed to walk in the revelation that God is so much more diverse and has much greater capacity than our finite minds have ever or will ever be able to grasp.

When getting ready for a new construction project like the Sears Tower in Chicago, do the builders start by putting the steel beams of a building together and erect it right on a bare piece of ground? No, they start with digging down deep. They may spend months or even years preparing the foundation so that what can be seen from above is supported by something firm and steadfast below. The purpose of a good foundation is so that through all the pressure of the elements of wind and snow, even the moving of the earth itself, the building will stand. Look at an example Jesus used:

Whoever comes to Me, and hears My sayings and does them, I will show you whom he is like: He is like a man building a house, who dug deep and laid the foundation on the rock. And when the flood arose, the stream beat vehemently against that house, and could not shake it, for it was founded on the rock. But he who heard and did nothing is like a man who built a house on the earth without a foundation, against which the stream beat vehemently; and immediately it fell. And the ruin of that house was great." (Luke 6:47-49 NKJV)

Jesus stated, "Whoever hears My sayings and does them" (Luke 6:47 NKJV). Hearing is a verb meaning it has action, not just with the natural ear but with the attention given to living it out. The Word shows us how Jesus approached the training of people. He had to focus on that which would support the work to come. That work would be seen by the world so He focused first on the leaders, not on the masses. The main reason today that we do not see the retention of new believers from massive meetings is that we have not spent the time to build the foundation of people to lead new believers, let alone the masses. Look at the parable of the sower:

Listen! Behold, a sower went out to sow. And it happened, as he sowed, that some seed fell by the wayside; and the birds of the air came and devoured it. Some fell on stony ground, where it did not have much earth; and immediately it sprang up because it had no depth of earth. But when the sun was up it was scorched, and because it had no root it withered away. And some seed fell among thorns; and the thorns grew up and choked it, and it yielded no crop. But other seed fell on good ground and yielded a crop that sprang up, increased and produced: some thirtyfold, some sixty, and some a hundred. (Mark 4:3-8 NKJV)

Now let's examine this. The seed that fell by the wayside was consumed, there was nothing to support its growth. Then that which fell on stony ground, though it came up was unable to grow roots and was scorched. The seed that fell among the thorns was choked out. Only the seed that fell on the good ground yielded a crop of increase. Satan will fight us at every level where we have not prepared ourselves to handle, and he will succeed.

What if the farmer in the parable took the time to till the wayside, the rocky and the thorny soils? There would have been increase! I think we all understand that the reception in the heart is up to the person being sown into. Many times, receiving it is not the problem. Rather, it's having enough laborers to go forth and continue to equip others. It is up to the body of Christ to mentor and make disciples and see results in the life of new believers. The days of the Body of Christ waiting for someone else to do the work and "pray" for God to send laborers are over! We are those laborers and we must rise up and do what we have been assigned to do.

When you read through Acts, do you see the church praying for laborers? After Peter and John were released from jail, they went to their brethren and the prayer went like this:

Now, Lord, look on their threats, and grant to Your servants that with all boldness they may speak Your word, by stretching out Your hand to heal, and that signs and wonders may be done through the name of Your holy Servant Jesus". (Acts 4:29-30 NKJV)

They did not pray that God would send someone else. They prayed that they would be granted boldness to speak the Word of God and become the laborers! Think about this with all that is at our disposal, should we not be raising up more people to lead the Body of Christ than ever before?

Let's rise up and use the tools that God has placed in our hands through technology, with the principles Jesus set out, and reach more than ever before. Let us rise up to personally steward those whom God has added to the church. Not because someone made us do it but because God has given us His boldness to speak the Word into the lives of people and bring about change in the earth.

ASSOCIATION

Jesus made a regular practice of being with the twelve. He did not use the training that we have available today through seminaries and Bible College. He made it simple by staying in regular contact with them. Don't misunderstand, I am not saying we should forego formal means of training and education, but we must not think that this is all that one needs to qualify for the ministry. Truly, the way to know people will not come mass meetings, but relationship is through times that there may only be a few. Are we becoming exclusive? No, we are responsible for those God adds through salvation. We can only affect change in a disciples life by taking the time as Jesus did to both personally address the questions of a disciple and live out before them a life of integrity by the Word.

The following day, Jesus wanted to go to Galilee, and He found Philip and said to him, "Follow Me." (John 1:43 NKJV)

The word follow is akoloutheo, which in the Greek means to be in the same way with, to accompany specifically as a disciple. Jesus was not just saying "follow me to my home." "He was placing on them a call to discipleship, not just to learn doctrine from the Scholastic or mental point of perspective but see how I live." Today there are great teachings on discipleship, but how many are living out the example so that their disciples can see it walked out?

Understand that results are not instant. The sad fact is that we as leaders and believers want microwave disciples. Regrettably many do not stay long enough to see the results of this type of training. But those who persevere by remaining active in discipleship and making disciples of others will see fruit that remains and multiplies.

Here I want to address making that association of disciple and the one who disciple others real. In modern day ministry, it is too often neglected. Following up personally with people is a rare occurrence in the Body of Christ today. We have bought into the lie that people would be offended if we stop in or make a personal phone call. Or we have made ourselves busy with things that really have no eternal value. Jesus had a follow up ministry! Read Luke 19:1-10, where Jesus said, "I must stay at your house." Zacchaeus went ahead to see Jesus, at Samaria, Jesus came into contact with a woman whom he asked for a drink and proceeded to tell her about her relationships and personal life. This opened the door for her to put faith in the Messiah and immediately she went to town to invite others to experience the Savior.

> *The woman then left her waterpot, went her way into the city, and said to the men, "Come, see a Man who told me all things that I ever did. Could this be the Christ?" Then they went out of the city and came to Him. (John 4:28-30 NKJV)*

The ministry did not stop with this woman's conversion and the invitation to others. Jesus did not say, "You know, I have a pretty busy travel schedule and I need to get back to Jerusalem to be crucified so you are on your own from here". Of course not--

let's look further at the Word.

> *And many of the Samaritans of that city believed in Him because of the word of the woman who testified, "He told me all that I ever did." So, when the Samaritans had come to Him, they urged Him to stay with them; and He stayed there two days. And many more believed because of His own word. Then they said to the woman, "Now we believe, not because of what you said, for we ourselves have heard Him and we know that this is indeed the Christ, the Savior of the world." Now after the two days He departed from there and went to Galilee. (John 4:39-43 NKJV)*

Jesus took the time to bring their understanding to a level that they could continue to grow. The scriptures tell us that Jesus stayed two days. They came to experience Him because the word of the woman drew them but the Word of Jesus kept them. Isaiah 55:11, which says, "So shall be My word that goes forth from My mouth, it shall not return to me void."

God sent Phillip down to Samaria to preach Christ to them and many heeded the message and were saved, delivered and healed. Now look at the follow-up:

> *Now when the apostles who were at Jerusalem heard that Samaria had received the word of God, they sent Peter and John to them, who, when they had come down, prayed for them that they might receive the Holy Spirit. For as yet He had fallen upon none of them. They had only been baptized in the name of the Lord Jesus. Then they laid hands on them, and they received the Holy Spirit. (Acts 8:14-17 NKJV)*

They were not just left on their own to get understanding, there was a follow up team. How did they ever get the idea that this was a necessary next step? He told the disciples, "And you will also bear witness, because you have been with me from the beginning." (John 15:27 NKJV) They were simply bearing witness as to how to carry forth the work of God by personal example, following up and living the doctrine, not just preaching it.

> *Every member of the community of faith had a part to fulfill in this ministry. But this they could only do as they themselves were trained and inspired. As long as Jesus was with them in the flesh, he was the Leader, but thereafter, it was necessary for those in the church to assume this leadership. Again, this meant that Jesus had to train them to do it, which involved His own constant personal association with a few chosen men. (Coleman 48)*

When the Body of Christ really becomes doers of this example, we will see the work complete, and the church with its assignment complete will be caught away to be with Jesus in eternity. Hallelujah!!!!

CONSECRATION

The next area I want to focus on in Jesus' pattern of evangelism and discipleship is that of consecration, being set apart. Too often there is no real separation between what the world looks like and what the church looks like. Many today want to be disciples on their own terms having the appearance that they have paid a price to be in a place of prominence. The price we must pay to walk in the true blessing is that of obedience to all the Word, not just the parts we like. The need for distinction between what is pure, biblical and holy is needed now more than ever. Jesus said not all who say to me "Lord, Lord" will enter the Kingdom. (Matthew 7:21 NKJV)

I think about the Apostle Paul who was used so powerfully of God. When he was Saul, persecuting the church, he met Jesus on the road to Damascus and there were no excuses. Saul responded "what do you want me to do?". We can see through his letters to the Corinthians Paul wrote, "you are not your own" (1 Corinthians 6:19 NKJV) and he told the Galatians, "I have been crucified with Christ" (Galatians 2:20 NKJV). In other words, he was set apart. Paul did not follow Jesus on his own terms, he immediately forsook all to give his life for Jesus.

> *But what things were gain to me, these I have counted loss for Christ. Yet indeed I also count all things loss for the excellence of the knowledge of Christ Jesus my Lord, for whom I have suffered the loss of all things, and count them as rubbish, that I may gain Christ and be found in Him, not having my own righteousness, which is from the law, but that which is through faith in Christ, the righteousness which is from God by faith; that I may know Him and the power of His resurrection, and the fellowship of His sufferings, being conformed to His death, if, by any means, I may attain to the resurrection from the dead. (Philippians 3:7-11 NKJV)*

To see lasting and enduring transformation, we must follow the example of Paul. Once Jesus touched his life, he walked counting it all loss: counting everything else as trash, being found only in Jesus.

Let's take some time looking at the original disciples that followed Jesus, who understood that He was the One to fulfill redemption. As the end drew closer, the pressure of being set apart was too much for many to bear. We see in John 6:66, that many of the disciples went back and did not walk with Him any more. When sharing the gospel with people, let's be sure we are not sharing a gospel of convenience. The tag line sometimes looks like this- "try Jesus He'll make your life better". We have too often simplified the message of the cross into a self-serving message of inspiration, without giving people the revelation of true relationship. This relationship requires repentance from sin and a forsaking all to follow Him. Yes, Jesus will make your life better but not like our world defines it: superficial nonsense of brighter smiles, fresher breath, more money, better marriages, or the perfect physique.

> *Jesus answered them, "Do you now believe? Indeed the hour is coming, yes, has now come, that you will be scattered, each to his own, and will leave Me alone. And yet I am not alone, because the Father is with Me. These things I have spoken to you, that in Me you may have peace. In the world you [1]will have tribulation; but be of good cheer, I have overcome the world." (John 16:31- 33 NKJV)*

In Jesus' own words, He said that in this world you will have tribulation. Let's focus on that word tribulation for a moment. In the Greek, it can be pictured as intense crushing pressure. The Roman government was known for cruel and unusual forms of torture. They would often take Christians being persecuted and use them as game for wild animals in the colosseum or as human torches. One form of torture was to lay a person flat, bound with ropes, and lower a boulder down on them in small increments. This was done until the person either renounced Christ or was crushed to death. Make no mistake--we win if we are killed for our faith! Here we must ask ourselves, have we made disciples that are separated to the point of not turning back?

There is so much more to being set apart than the outward blessings and benefits. We must truly be set apart in order to see our lives transformed by Him. He said, "If you love Me, keep my commandments." (John 14:15) To keep means to guard, to keep an eye on, to prevent from escaping, to hold fast. There is action required of us if we are to show the world we love Him. Diligence is required to be one who is set apart, consecrated to God. Are we truly prepared to pay the price of full obedience to His Word without preconceived terms, plans, or motives? Will we become the servant of all?

IMPARTATION

"Just as the Son of Man did not come to be served, but to serve, and to give His life a ransom for many." (Matthew 20:28 NKJV)

Jesus gave of Himself to them. He became servant of all in living and giving Himself to His disciples. Jesus gave His true love to His disciples and to the world. His love was unconditional from the perspective that He did not do it to get something from them in return. As a servant of all, our lives must be lived as those who impart, not those who always consume.

How think ye? If a man have a hundred sheep, and one of them be gone astray, doth he not leave the ninety and nine, and goeth into the mountains, and seeketh that which is gone astray? And if so be that he find it, verily I say unto you, he rejoiceth more of that sheep, than of the ninety and nine which went not astray. Even so it is not the will of your Father which is in heaven, that one of these little ones should perish (Matthew 18:12-14 KJV).

He gave them instruction through parables and through His daily life. He had to go after those who were straying, those who were lost and those who were hurting. When Jesus saw a woman was bound, in His compassion, He loosed her from that infirmity. (Luke 13:16 NKJV) But Jesus did not do it all Himself; He imparted power to the twelve and sent them out, then the seventy also.

After these things the Lord appointed seventy others also, and sent them two by two before His face into every city and place where He Himself was about to go. Then He said to them, "The harvest truly is great, but the laborers are few; therefore pray the Lord of the harvest to send out laborers into His harvest. Go your way; behold, I send you out as lambs among wolves. Carry neither money bag, knapsack, nor sandals; and greet no one along the road. But whatever house you enter, first say, 'Peace to this house.' And if a son of peace is there, your peace will rest on it; if not, it will return to you. And remain in the same house, eating and drinking such things as they give, for the laborer is worthy of his wages. Do not go from house to house. Whatever city you enter, and they receive you, eat such things as are set before you. And heal the sick there, and say to them, 'The kingdom of God has come near to you.' But whatever city you enter, and they do not receive you, go out into its streets and say, 'The very dust of your city which clings to us we wipe off against you. Nevertheless, know this, that the kingdom of God has come near you.' But I say to you that it will be more tolerable in that Day for Sodom than for that city. "Woe to you, Chorazin! Woe to you, Bethsaida! For if the mighty works which were done in you had been done in Tyre and Sidon, they would have repented long ago, sitting in sackcloth and ashes. But it will be more tolerable for Tyre and Sidon at the judgment than for you. And you, Capernaum, who are exalted to heaven, will be brought down to Hades. He who hears you hears Me, he who rejects you rejects Me, and he who rejects Me rejects Him who sent Me." Then the seventy returned with joy, saying, "Lord, even the demons are subject to us in Your name." (Luke 10:1-17 NKJV)

Who are we imparting into? Whose life will be better as a result of the impartation God gives them through our lives?

DEMONSTRATION

Jesus demonstrated for the disciples not just the spiritual side of things, but also the balance of living everyday life in the midst of doing the will of the Father. Unfortunately, I have experienced personally my life getting out of balance. Remember going to one extreme with spiritual or ministry emphasis to the neglect of family, finances, physical rest, and so on will lead to nothing but regret.

The Holy Spirit will not balance your checkbook. He will not fulfill your responsibility as a husband to listen to and care for your wife and children. It is your responsibility to find and live balanced in the ministry and family God has given you stewardship of. At one time, I had so neglected my physical care, I herniated a disc in my back and almost became paralyzed. I have bounced checks because I was "too busy" to give proper attention to that practical side of life. We must not ruin our testimony just because we think we are being spiritual. Part of our witness is being good stewards in every area of life.

Jesus was careful to not damage His testimony as being from the Father. He showed his disciples the importance of intimacy with God through prayer and fellowship. God's presence was a vital key to His success in every area of His life. We must live out and demonstrate an attitude of one who "seeks first the Kingdom of God and His righteousness." (Matthew 6:33 NKJV) As important as caring for the Body of Christ is, being only known for this will not count before God. Raises, big offerings, having big meetings, impressive buildings and the like have no real value in light of eternity. But when we spend time being intimate with Him, we have the wisdom to take care of all those other things and will live out and demonstrate the principles of God to those we lead.

Look at Jesus' response to times of stress such as John the Baptist's death. Upon hearing the news, He departed to a deserted place and though the multitudes followed Him, he sent them away and spent time in intimate fellowship with God.

And straightway Jesus constrained his disciples to get into a ship, and to go before him unto the other side, while he sent the multitudes away. And when he had sent the multitudes away, he went up into a mountain apart to pray: and when the evening was come, he was there alone. (Matthew 14:22-23 NKJV)

In John 6:15, when the people wanted to come and make Jesus king, His response made it clear where His focus and devotion were: He departed by Himself to pray. After healing the man with the withered hand on the Sabbath, the scriptures say He withdrew. Sometimes it is important that we withdraw from the masses and the business of life, and get one on one with God so that the anointing we walk in does not get diminished or our focus lost. Consider these scriptures:

However, the report went around concerning Him all the more; and great multitudes came together to hear, and to be healed by Him of their infirmities. So He Himself often withdrew into the wilderness and prayed. (Luke 5:15-16 NKJV)

Jesus even took the disciples aside.

Then the apostles gathered to Jesus and told Him all things, both what they had done and what they had taught. And He said to them, "Come aside by yourselves to a deserted place and rest a while." For there were many coming and going, and they did not even have time to eat. So, they departed to a deserted place in the boat by themselves. (Mark 6:30-32 NKJV)

If Jesus set the example for the disciples to come apart, we must do the same. Taking an honest look and having a friend of accountability will help keep us from being blindsided. If we will follow His pattern, we will see greater miracles and a greater anointing in our lives. One last thing on this…your family will thank God that you did!

DELEGATION

Let's attempt to bring balance to the matter of delegation. Because of past bad experiences, some are unwilling to delegate even the most mundane tasks. On the other extreme, others push believers out before they know much about walking in integrity and in the power of the Spirit. All too soon, they are either burned out or become puffed up with pride.

The Apostle Paul gave such practical wisdom concerning the matter of delegation in leadership.

A bishop (overseer) then must be blameless, the husband of one wife, temperate, sober-minded, of good behavior, hospitable, able to teach; not given to wine, not violent, not greedy for money, but gentle, not quarrelsome, not covetous; one who rules his own house well, having his children in submission with all reverence (for if a man does not know how to rule his own house, how will he take care of the church of God?); not a novice, lest being puffed up with pride he fall into the same condemnation as the devil. Moreover, he must have a good testimony among those who are outside, lest he fall into reproach and the snare of the devil. (2 Timothy 3:2-7 NKJV)

Although I will discuss the matter of who's qualified for leadership, I wanted to target here the matter of delegation in the church. If you ask one to do certain things too soon, they fall. But Paul also makes it clear, that if the other principles are lined up and you have instruction from God, it would be a mistake to not place them in a position of delegated responsibility. Think about how Jesus did not send out the disciples immediately. They spent extensive time with Jesus before they received their first assignment to go out and proclaim the Kingdom of God.

Jesus' method was to get the disciples into a vital experience with God, and to show them how He worked, before telling them they had to do it (Coleman 79).

As He prepared them and was about to send them out, He did not just send them out without first giving them instructions. These instructions were no different than what He had been teaching and demonstrating for them all along but served as greater clarification of their mission. Jesus' assignment was very clear for the disciples.

And as you go, preach, saying, 'The kingdom of heaven is at hand.' Heal the sick, cleanse the lepers, raise the dead, cast out demons. Freely you have received, freely give. (Matthew 10:7-8 NKJV)

Freely you have received, freely give! Jesus did not want them to think that all that had taken place to this point was for their personal benefit. It is not what we get that makes the difference but what we give. I love a quote from Winston Churchill that says, "You make a living by what you get, you make a life by what you give". Look at the illustrations of Jesus in Mark 4.

And He said, "The kingdom of God is as if a man should scatter seed on the ground, and should sleep by night and rise by day, and the seed should sprout and grow, he himself does not know how. For the earth yields crops by itself: first the blade, then the head, after that the full grain in the head. But when the grain ripens, immediately he puts in the sickle, because the harvest has come." Then He said, "To what shall we liken the kingdom of God? Or with what parable shall we picture it? It is like a mustard seed which, when it is sown on the ground, is smaller than all the seeds on earth; but when it is sown, it grows up and becomes greater than all herbs, and shoots out large branches, so that the birds of the air may nest under its shade." (Mark 4:26-32 NKJV)

If we sit on what God has done in us and entrusted to us, we remain unproductive.

Verily, verily, I say unto you, except a corn of wheat fall into the ground and die, it abideth alone: but if it die, it bringeth forth much fruit. (John 12:24 KJV)

If we are to see the most out of our ministry, we must give what we have. We must be consistent to establish our leadership structure with true disciples of Jesus Christ and see fruit that will remain.

SUPERVISION

Many times, we have all been remiss in one of the six areas shared thus far, but failure in supervision will really come back to bite us if we neglect it. Generally, it is not what is expected of people that they do but what is inspected.

In Mark 6, after the twelve returned and in Luke 10, the seventy they came and reported to Jesus all they had done, all they saw, all they experienced. There will always be an accounting for our work and that's not bondage, it's wisdom! Without accountability, how could Jesus bring out the weaknesses, and how could the disciples get their questions answered?

I have found that it is important to focus on the following four areas.

1) Instruction
2) Discipline
3) Correction
4) Consequences

First, when training people, there must be instruction so that the task at hand becomes clear. Second, is discipline but not discipline as we have come to know the word. But discipline as Paul uses it in 1 Corinthians 9:27, "I discipline my body and bring it into subjection." In other words, there must be a pattern of regularity in our lives about that assignment. Third, as instruction is received and discipline practiced, where correction through supervision is necessary.

For example, this is the way you have been carrying out this assignment, now here are the areas of change that need to be made to optimize your efforts in this assignment.

If we will walk in the first three, we will be great disciples and leaders whom God can use, and we will never get to the last stage, that of punishment. The fourth area is consequence, this is an area of focus reserved for the rebellious, those who strive against sound wisdom and instruction given by those God has placed over us in the Lord.

Obey those who rule over you, and be submissive, for they watch out for your souls, as those who must give account. Let them do so with joy and not with grief, for that would be unprofitable for you. (Hebrews 13:17 NKJV)

It is of no benefit to those we lead for them to rebel, but it is of no benefit to us to leave them on their own and never inspect what is going on. I am not saying there is no grace, certainly there should be, but we cannot just assume that because we have given an assignment it has been completed. This is another area of balance: don't assume what was asked is what was done and don't micromanage. Facilitate an environment of growth and development that will outlast your time on this earth.

REPRODUCTION

As Jesus' time with the disciples came to a close, the element of making disciples came into play. As He began to wind down His time here on earth, He shifts His focus from fulfilling the will of God on the earth while He walked the earth to what His disciples would do after He left the earth.

I am the true vine, and My Father is the vinedresser. Every branch in Me that does not bear fruit He takes away; and every branch that bears fruit He prunes, that it may bear more fruit. You are already clean because of the word which I have spoken to you. Abide in Me, and I in you. As the branch cannot bear fruit of itself, unless it abides in the vine, neither can you, unless you abide in Me. "I am the vine, you are the branches. He who abides in Me, and I in him, bears much fruit; for without Me you can do nothing. If anyone does not abide in Me, he is cast out as a branch and is withered; and they gather them and throw them into the fire, and they are burned. If you abide in Me, and My words abide in you, you will ask what you desire, and it shall be done for you. By this My Father is glorified, that you bear much fruit; so you will be My disciples. (John 15:1-8 NKJV)

As we abide in Him, we cannot help but bear fruit and see great multiplication and reproduction of the Word of God in the earth. In the Garden of Gethsemane, Jesus prayed, "I do not pray for these alone (the disciples), but also for those who will believe in Me through their word." (John 17:20 NKJV) After the crucifixion and resurrection, Jesus gave further instruction as to the assignment that they were to carry out from that point forward.

And Jesus came and spoke to them, saying, "All authority has been given to Me in heaven and on earth. Go therefore and make disciples of all the nations, baptizing them in the name of the Father and of the Son and of the Holy Spirit, teaching them to observe all things that I have commanded you; and lo, I am with you always, even to the end of the age." Amen. (Matthew 28:18-20 NKJV)

Go into all the world and preach the gospel to every creature. He who believes and is baptized will be saved; but he who does not believe will be condemned. And these signs will follow those who believe: In My name they will cast out demons; they will speak with new tongues; they will take up serpents; and if they drink anything deadly, it will by no means hurt them; they will lay hands on the sick, and they will recover." So then, after the Lord had spoken to them, He was received up into heaven, and sat down at the right hand of God. And they went out and preached everywhere, the Lord working with them and confirming the word through the accompanying signs. Amen. (Mark 16:15-20 NKJV)

With the assignment clear and time certain, they were to wait in Jerusalem for the power to complete the will of the Father and be witnesses. He said He would not leave them orphans but would send them a Helper, the Holy Spirit, the one called alongside to carry out Jesus' ministry through their lives.

It is very important that we talk about what it means to be a disciple. When we look at definitions of the word from the dictionary, we begin to see a picture that can be confirmed through the Word. Simply put, a disciple is one who accepts and assists in spreading the doctrines of another. To paraphrase, "A disciple is also defined as one of the twelve in the inner circle of Christ's followers according to the Gospel accounts. Finally, a disciple is one who is a convinced adherent (one who is enthusiastic or passionate about) a school or individual."

Regarding reproduction in the Body of Christ, we must look for those who are going to be disciples in the true sense of the word. We must look for someone who is enthusiastic and passionate about the Word and hungry to be trained in righteousness. As we train and mentor people, we must realize that we train them for Jesus, not ourselves and not for our own gain. Yes, they will reflect us, but as Paul said "Follow me as I follow Christ." (1 Corinthians 11:1 NKJV) So, we want those we disciple to only follow the things that reflect Jesus in us.

3

WHAT IS YOUR FOCUS?

As we have discussed, God's heart is to bring fallen man to the place of redemption, and He set the pattern through His son. In the next chapters, we will bring this into modern application and practical instruction on how to effect change in the Body of Christ today. From Jesus' ministry we see how important and valuable it is to reach and equip people.

> *Then all the tax collectors and the sinners drew near to Him to hear Him. And the Pharisees and scribes complained, saying, "This Man receives sinners and eats with them." So, He spoke this parable to them, saying:" What man of you, having a hundred sheep, if he loses one of them, does not leave the ninety-nine in the wilderness, and go after the one which is lost until he finds it? And when he has found it, he lays it on his shoulders, rejoicing. And when he comes home, he calls together his friends and neighbors, saying to*

them, 'Rejoice with me, for I have found my sheep which was lost!' I say to you that likewise there will be more joy in heaven over one sinner who repents than over ninety-nine just persons who need no repentance. (Luke 15:1-7 NKJV)

Jesus spent much of His time with people--most of whom the Body of Christ today would just as soon avoid. If we are going to grow successful ministries, we must pay attention to the needs of people. We must be willing to go to anyone, anywhere, at any time. I want to encourage believers to make sure to be found faithful in this assignment.

The five-fold ministry is responsible to equip the saints for the work of the ministry. Every member of the Body of Christ has the responsibility to disciple and train up new converts and help care for the body.

For as the body is one and has many members, but all the members of that one body, being many, are one body, so also is Christ. For by one Spirit we were all baptized into one body—whether Jews or Greeks, whether slaves or free—and have all been made to drink into one Spirit. For in fact the body is not one member but many. If the foot should say, "Because I am not a hand, I am not of the body," is it therefore not of the body? And if the ear should say, "Because I am not an eye, I am not of the body," is it therefore not of the body? If the whole body were an eye, where would be the hearing? If the whole were hearing, where would bethe smelling? But now God has set the members, each one of them, in the body just as He pleased. And if they were all one member, where would the body be? 20 But now indeed there are many members, yet one body. And the eye cannot say to the hand, "I have no need of you"; nor again the head to the feet, "I have no need of you." No, much rather, those members of the body which seem to be weaker are necessary. And those members of the body which we think to be less honorable, on these we bestow greater honor; and our unpresentable parts have greater modesty, but our presentable parts have no need. But God composed the body, having given greater honor to that part which lacks it, that there should be no [li]schism in the body, but that the members should have the same care for one another. And if one member suffers, all the members suffer with it; or if one member is honored, all the members rejoice with it. (1 Corinthians 12:12-26 NKJV)

You must partner with God so that none of those He has made you steward over is lost. We must look at people the way that God does: through the realm of the Spirit and not just through the natural. I believe many may have backed off the personal approach because of those who have wasted their time and efforts. I understand there are some who will refuse to do what you counsel them to do. But never allow the disobedience of others to become the excuse you use for not getting out and going to people, choosing instead to stay closed up in an office or prayer closet somewhere.

You never know if the person you are ministering to may be someone great in the kingdom of heaven. If you are the leader of a church, you must set the example of what you want people to do, not just preach it to them all the time. As we train people to enter into realms of their gifts and callings, they will minister to people that you will never be able to touch.

Looking at the parable above in Luke 15, let us look for a minute at the natural. You see it all the time on the news- if an animal is in crisis, the owner goes to great lengths to save its life. In Matthew 6:26 (NKJV), Jesus said, "Look at the birds of the air, for they neither sow nor reap nor gather into barns; yet your heavenly Father feeds them. Are you not much more valuable than they?" God has placed a higher value on people than we truly understand. His valuation of people is higher than anything we may have going on in our churches. Without reaching people, ministry becomes dissatisfying. If personality and teaching ability were enough to build and sustain a strong ministry, there would be more mega church ministries in the world. Generally speaking, people are not going to be a participating, invested part of a local body just because the teaching is inspiring, and the pastor's personality is friendly and relevant.

People must also be cared for, and their personal ministry needs met. They need to be equipped to a point of confidence that inspires them to fulfill the Great Commission of preaching the Gospel to all creatures and making disciples of all nations. We must inspire people to action and has them begin to take a personal interest in the body. Remember, the concrete and mortar that stand on a piece of dirt are not God's building, the people are. Paul writes, "For we are God's fellow workers; you are God's field, you are God's building". (1 Corinthians 3:9 NKJV)

If we are content with where we are and what we have, shame on us. God is a God of increase and change; He does not change, but He is changing us from glory to glory by His Spirit. God wants us to pursue excellence in ministry. No matter what size the church, we are called to be fruitful, faithful stewards of the people God has given us.

> He also said to His disciples: There was a certain rich man who had a steward, and an accusation was brought to him that this man was wasting his goods. "So, he called him and said to him, 'what is this that I hear about you? Give an account of your stewardship, for you can no longer be a steward...He who is faithful in what is least is faithful also in what is much; and he who is unjust in what is least is unjust in much. (Luke 16:1-2, 10 NKJV)

How often today do people leave a church, and no one ever contacts them to find out why? Recently, I did the funeral of a family member who lived a long, full life. I had been asked several years ago to do the funeral when the time came for this man to go home to be with the Lord. The church that they were a part of for many years had not been tending to and following up with them. On the day of the funeral, I noticed a minister in the room, and being a fellow preacher, I went and introduced myself. What followed brought tears to my eyes and great sadness to my heart. He regrettably admitted, "We really dropped the ball in the care of your family member." You could tell this really grieved him, and I am sure he could tell it bothered me. Unfortunately, this is a common, regular pattern in the church. As leaders, you and I must build a team of people around us to be sure that no one falls through the cracks regardless of age, circumstance, or how long or short they have been with the church.

God is much more concerned with people than with money or with process. We must be faithful stewards of God's money, but how much more should we be faithful stewards of the true riches of the lives that God has given us the responsibility to touch, care for and disciple? God is interested in the whole man. If we don't keep regular contact with people through an environment of discipleship, we will not know when they face personal crisis. We will have no way of knowing when their walk with God is struggling. Ministry is more than the ability to bring a great message in our services. It is also the ability to meet the needs of your sheep 24/7 (No, I am not saying you alone must do that! In a later chapter we will talk about how to accomplish this through your church body.)

FRUIT THAT REMAINS

Before developing this thought fully, I want to share an illustration God stirred in my heart. I was thinking how God made men and women different when it comes to children. For women there is a very different connection than that of men. I believe the main reason is that even though it takes a man and woman to conceive, the woman carries the child in the womb until that child can live outside of the environment it was conceived.

As I thought about this, it began to dawn on me that maybe we as the church have not viewed the new babe in Christ the right way. We celebrate when someone gives their heart to Christ, and it is indeed, a wonderful thing that should be celebrated. But can you imagine if we started to view that as the moment of the conception of their faith and then the church cared for them as a pregnant woman does her child? I think we would have a greater care and desire to nurture new believers if we took greater personal interest in their ability to survive and thrive.

Jesus spoke about the fruit of our lives being much and remaining, but too often today that is not what we see. Often people who respond to altar calls are never seen again after that service. If the Body of Christ is doing its God-given assignment, to make disciples, we will see fruit that remains and grows. Certainly, the person who responds has a responsibility to do something with what they have received, but if we are not making disciples then we have fallen short of the call.

You have not chosen Me, but I have chosen you and I have appointed you [I have planted you], that you might go and bear fruit and keep on bearing, and that your fruit may be lasting [that it may remain, abide], so that whatever you ask the Father in My Name [as presenting all that I AM], He may give it to you. (John 15:16 AMPC)

You didn't choose me. I chose you. I appointed you to go and produce fruit that will last, so that the Father will give you whatever you ask for, using my name. I command you to love each other. (John 15:16-17 NLT)

You did not choose Me, but I chose you and appointed you that you should go and bear fruit, and that your fruit should remain, that whatever you ask the Father in My name He may give you. (John 15:16-17 NKJV)

The word "remain" in the Greek is the word meno (men'-o) It is a primary verb meaning to stay in a given place, state, relation or expectancy. The Body of Christ under God the Father and Jesus are responsible to plant, tend and harvest souls. We are responsible to do everything possible to see fruit remain. God does not want us to have great services and small groups that never grow or events that just entertain. God wants to see that the fruit harvested remains. Let's look at a discovery of Solomon from the book of Proverbs.

> *I went by the field of the lazy man, and by the vineyard of the man devoid of understanding; And there it was, all overgrown with thorns; Its surface was covered with nettles; Its stonewall was broken down. When I saw it, I considered it well; I looked on it and received instruction: A little sleep, a little slumber, A little folding of the hands to rest; So, shall your poverty come like a prowler, And your need like an armed man. (Proverbs 24:30-34 NKJV)*

Solomon here talks about the instruction he received when passing the field of the lazy man. It was overgrown, untended, the curse was on it; this man was not being a good steward of what he had. The stone wall of protection for the crop was broken down, thus allowing wild animals in, allowing consumption and destruction of what grew.

Notice here that it does not say the ground was not good; it says that as a result of a slothful attitude, poverty came in like a prowler, need and lack came in like an armed man. A lack of focus, gratitude, and just plain work had taken its toll on this field and crop.

The Body of Christ today has grown lazy when it comes to tending the fields that God has given us to steward. This is one of the key reasons why the prosperity of God has not been able to flow freely into our ministries and growth has leveled off or declined. We, like Solomon, must receive the instruction of the Word, "A little sleep, a little slumber, A little folding of the hands to rest; So, shall poverty come." We must be diligent about tending the field and fruit that God has given us in the Body of Christ. Blessed are you who sow beside all waters, who send out freely the feet of the ox and the donkey. (Isaiah 32:20 NKJV)

Notice that Isaiah declares to send out freely. Genesis 8:22 reads, "While the earth remains, Seedtime and harvest, Cold and heat, winter and summer, and day and night Shall not cease." In our ministries it is important that we seek to always apply the principles of seedtime and harvest, without the seed of care for the flock, we will never see a harvest, without diligence to be good stewards of the Body of Christ, could we hear these words?

> ...'Depart from Me, you cursed, into the everlasting fire prepared for the devil and his angels: for I was hungry and you gave Me no food; I was thirsty and you gave Me no drink; I was a stranger and you did not take Me in, naked and you did not clothe Me, sick and in prison and you did not visit Me...' 'Assuredly, I say to you, inasmuch as you did not do it to one of the least of these, you did not do it to Me'. (Matthew 25:41-43, 45 NKJV)

The way we treat the people that God puts under our care will determine the words that we hear on that day. Promotion comes from God so maybe we will be permitted in, but there will be no reward for our labor if we have not diligently pursued with passion the assignment God has given us.

KNOWING AND TENDING GOD'S FLOCK

Over many years pursuing people, I have visited with many, many people who had been in ministries of all types and sizes who said that no one had ever visited them. As ministers of the Gospel, those with the assignment of the office of Pastor must make sure that there are systems in place that help us know and observe the state of those who call our ministry home.

Be diligent to know the state of your flocks, and attend to your herds; for riches are not forever, nor does a crown endure to all generations. When the hay is removed, and the tender grass shows itself, and the herbs of the mountains are gathered in, the lambs will provide your clothing, and the goats the price of a field; You shall have enough goats' milk for your food, for the food of your household, and the nourishment of your maidservants. (Proverbs 27:23-27 NKJV)

The word "know" is the Hebrew word "yada" which means to observe, care, instruct, recognize and correct. We must equip people to serve with us so that we can know and recognize our people and their needs. To complete the work that God has given the Body of Christ for the end time harvest, we must build up the people through knowing and caring for them. Temporal things that we might consider important will not last. However, if we take care to being diligent with those God has made us stewards of, we will have more than enough. Look at the principle above in verse 27 that reveals you shall have enough. The word "day" meaning enough, sufficient, too much. If we do not have enough, we should deeply, thoughtfully begin the examination of our ministry by asking some questions. Have we given diligent attention to knowing our flock?

When we are faithful with the people, in addition to following the principles of the Word, the windows of heaven will be open over us. We will walk in heavenly provision and walk in a level of prosperity that has not been seen.

COMMAND TO DILIGENCE

In Proverbs 27:23 a command to diligence to our calling. This dictate is to both the husbandman (Senior Pastor) and to the shepherd (associates and support staff, small group leaders) in the local church. We must not live in idleness or complacency or even focus our attention on well-meaning but misdirected efforts. We must rightly and fully know the face and business of our flock. We must have an eye to it ourselves and not entrust it to others with no accountability. "Be sober, be vigilant; because your adversary the devil walks about like a roaring lion, seeking whom he may devour." (1 Peter 5:8 NKJV) Remember Solomon's observations, "a little sleep, a little slumber so shall your poverty come like a prowler." (Proverbs 24:23 NKJV)

REASONS TO FOLLOW THE COMMAND

Remember that maintenance is easier than having to continually rebuild. Think of David, though he had been anointed king, he still looked to the good care of his father's flock, 1 Chronicles 27:29-31. Our labor is not in making grass come forth to feed the flock. But we must have the herd gathered together so that as God brings forth the tender grass, they are there to feed. God has done His part and we must do ours.

> The lambs will provide your clothing, and the goats the price of a field; You shall have enough (day-enough, sufficient, too much) goats' milk for your food, for the food of your household, and the nourishment of your maidservants. (Proverbs 27:26-27 NKJV)

Taking care of people means that there will be plenty for us to meet our personal needs, the needs of our family and those around us. It means that the work of God will go forth unhindered and there will not be any lack in the local church. We don't look to them for our finances but, rather, in fulfilling the assignment of God the blessing of God is at work in our lives. We must be diligent and industrious about our business so that we will have plenty. Having care for the flock means that we can see into their lives to bring comfort and correction. When we equip, so that the Body of Christ is built up and edified, then we will see the greatest breakthrough and this gospel will be preached in all the earth.

> *Therefore, take heed to yourselves and to all the flock, among which the Holy Spirit has made you overseers, to shepherd the church of God which He purchased with His own blood. (Acts 20:28 NKJV)*

> *The elders who are among you I exhort, I who am a fellow elder and a witness of the sufferings of Christ, and also a partaker of the glory that will be revealed: Shepherd the flock of God which is among you, serving as overseers, not by compulsion but willingly, not for dishonest gain but eagerly; nor as being lords over those entrusted to you, but being examples to the flock; and when the Chief Shepherd appears, you will receive the crown of glory that does not fade away. (1 Peter 5:1-4 NKJV)*

> *But we were gentle among you, just as a nursing mother cherishes her own children. So, affectionately longing for you, we were well pleased to impart to you not only the gospel of God, but also our own lives, because you had become dear to us. (1 Thessalonians 2:7-9 NKJV)*

WHAT IS YOUR PASSION?

Passion is defined as an intense, driving, or overmastering feeling, conviction, or ardent affection. It is a strong liking or desire for or devotion to some activity, object, or concept. Passion is an object of desire or deep interest, meaning intense emotion compelling action. My passion is to see that once evangelism has taken place that those who commit their lives to Christ get connected in the local body and get equipped to be disciples who make disciples of all nations.

What is the atmosphere of your ministry? Are people excited about going out with the tools you equip them with and building the body? Are they expecting that you will do the work of the ministry? The atmosphere of expectation will determine the direction of your congregation. Do the leaders in your life have a mentor relationship with you to give you counsel? It is important they have the right to counsel you and give you instruction in life. We all need to be mentored just as consistently as we mentor others.

Where is your focus? Broken focus will cause you to have no true direction in doing what the Word commands. The bottom line for the five-fold ministry is that if we are not equipping the saints for the work of the ministry, we have failed to carry out our assignment. Even more, there is a burning inside of those called to the five-fold ministry to fulfill the call, and nothing else will satisfy.

Passion is often revealed by our conversation, action and relationships. As the old saying goes, birds of a feather flock together. What you say and do, as well those who are closest to you reveals much about your pursuits and your passion. Jesus' passion and compassion was for those who were "like sheep having no shepherd." Jesus made disciples and started by calling Peter.

So it was, as the multitude pressed about Him to hear the word of God, that He stood by the Lake of Gennesaret, and saw two boats standing by the lake; but the fishermen had gone from them and were washing their nets. Then He got into one of the boats, which was Simon's, and asked him to put out a little from the land. And He sat down and taught the multitudes from the boat. When He had stopped speaking, He said to Simon, "Launch out into the deep and let down your nets for a catch." But Simon answered and said to Him, "Master, we have toiled all night and caught nothing; nevertheless, at Your word I will let down the net." And when they had done this, they caught a great number of fish, and their net was breaking. So, they signaled to their partners in the other boat to come and help them. And they came and filled both the boats, so that they began to sink. When Simon Peter saw it, he fell down at Jesus' knees, saying, "Depart from me, for I am a sinful man, O Lord!" For he and all who were with him were astonished at the catch of fish which they had taken; and so also were James and John, the sons of Zebedee, who were partners with Simon. And Jesus said to Simon, "Do not be afraid. From now on you will catch men." So when they had brought their boats to land, they forsook all and followed Him. (Luke 5:1-11 NKJV)

As Jesus passed on from there, He saw a man named Matthew sitting at the tax office. And He said to him, "Follow Me." So, he arose and followed Him. (Matthew 9:9 NKJV)

Jesus revealed to them there would be a price to discipleship. We must never be afraid to reveal to those we lead that to have something of worth there will always be a price to be paid. Sure, the price for salvation has been paid, but we must be willing to lay down our lives for the call to the Gospel.

When He had called the people to Himself, with His disciples also, He said to them, "Whoever desires to come after Me, let him deny himself, and take up his cross, and follow Me. For whoever desires to save his life will lose it, but whoever loses his life for My sake and the gospel's will save it. For what will it profit a man if he gains the whole world, and loses his own soul? Or what will a man give in exchange for his soul? For whoever is ashamed of Me and My words in this adulterous and sinful generation, of him the Son of Man also will be ashamed when He comes in the glory of His Father with the holy angels." (Mark 8:34-38 NKJV

Jesus demonstrated His heart to them so that they would see why He was here. Prior to this time, Israel had only been acquainted with the aspect of God as their judge. They had not known the true love and mercy of God as Jesus expressed on the earth. The old nature crept out from time to time as the disciples walked with Jesus on the earth.

Now it came to pass, when the time had come for Him to be received up, that He steadfastly set His face to go to Jerusalem, and sent messengers before His face. And as they went, they entered a village of the Samaritans, to prepare for Him. But they did not receive Him, because His face was set for the journey to Jerusalem. And when His disciples James and John saw this, they said, "Lord, do You want us to command fire to come down from heaven and consume them, just as Elijah did?" But He turned and rebuked them, and said, "You do not know what manner of spirit you are of. For the Son of Man did not come to destroy men's lives but to save them." And they went to another village. (Luke 9:51-56 NKJV)

Jesus, even at that late hour, had to set them straight and help them realize that God did not come to destroy but to save. He gave them many examples so that as they went out on their permanent assignments through life after His death and resurrection, they would not bring a reproach on His name. Jesus sent them out before his departure and gave them clear instruction.

And He called the twelve to Himself, and began to send them out two by two, and gave them power over unclean spirits. He commanded them to take nothing for the journey except a staff --no bag, no bread, no copper in their money belts--but to wear sandals, and not to put on two tunics. Also, He said to them, "In whatever place you enter a house, stay there till you depart from that place. And whoever will not receive you nor hear you, when you depart from there, shake off the dust under your feet as a testimony against them. Assuredly, I say to you, it will be more tolerable for Sodom and Gomorrah in the day of judgment than for that city!" So, they went out and preached that people should repent. And they cast out many demons, and anointed with oil many who were sick, and healed them. (Mark 6:7-13 NKJV)

He even instructed them what to do when they were not received, "shake the dust off your feet." But He never told them to stop! The results when we are diligently doing the command of the Father are not our responsibility. If we are doing the Word and teaching those who we lead to do the Word, we will see steady growth. If people choose to remain in the hardness of their hearts, then shake it off.

In over 25,000 visits I have personally made over the years, responses from some people have led me to shake the dust off and move on. I refuse to get bogged down with those who want to remain in their sin. Maybe the seed I have sown into their life will come up at some other time. The Apostle Paul said, one plants, one waters but God gives the increase (1 Corinthians 3:7-8 NKJV). You should never give up on people, but there is a time when you must move on because you are not received!

After the resurrection, it was time for the culmination of Jesus' mission and the beginning of the church that God has called into existence, the family that He desires. In Matthew 28:18-19, God gave a clear command to make disciples. The word "disciple" or "teach" in the King James Version reads is the Greek word matheteuo (math-ayt-yoo'-o) meaning to become a pupil or transitively, to disciple. This requires that we invest our lives and time into the life of someone who is a disciple. Sadly, it seems that there are few who want to be disciples in the true sense of the word, but that does not excuse us from our assignment. Evangelism and discipleship, and I must add revival are all inseparable. Usually, we see evangelism in an event rather than in a life. If big crusades and catchy gimmicks or seeker-friendly versions of the Gospel were all that was needed to reach people, the work would be complete, and we would be home with Jesus.

Large meetings and other tools should absolutely be used, but they must not be the only means or outreach for the Body of Christ. God is not looking for another program; He is looking for us to take personal responsibility for evangelism and discipleship. Too often we have had one without the other, but to fulfill the scriptural pattern of God's plan, they must supplement one another.

We need to completely change traditional thought about reaching the lost. This will require investing much more time, but let me ask you, how much is one soul worth to Jesus? Is our time more valuable than investing in eternity? Let's really dig deep and take time to pray, take time to set up a lunch appointment with someone, taking time to study to show yourself approved. Personal preparation and time will afford us the tools we need to make true disciples. When the questions come from a young believer, you must have stored up the wisdom of God stored up inside of you. Discipleship is not always going to be convenient, but it will always make a difference in the life of the disciple.

Whether you are a Senior Pastor or a member of the local church, is we must all be willing to follow Jesus' pattern. You do not need to spend every hour of every day with a person. Let us pursue those God has placed around us to bring them to and lead them in a fruitful life in Christ. As we continue in the next chapter, I want to talk to you about getting results and seeing God really move in the Body of Christ today.

4

GETTING RESULTS

When I started in the ministry, it became glaringly evident to me that there was a great deal of lack when it came to the adequate care of people in the church. I recall one time, just after I came on the staff of a church in my first full-time position in the ministry, I was there just a few weeks and I started to review the names of all the people that were on the absentee list of the church. I was shocked how many people who simply fell through the cracks.

In our churches, there are many who come and go who we really do not know, and when they disappear, no one ever finds out why. Maybe the family hit a rough financial place and are too proud to ask for help, maybe they lost a family member and got discouraged or maybe someone came into the church and was whispering, causing strife and division in the body. If we don't have a proactive approach to go after people then we will go through phases of growth and decline we cannot explain or understand.

Every church will face challenges, but we must stop giving satan a foothold by leaving the flock unattended. Don't buy the lie that you'll never face a problem in the ministry or a challenge to the body--that's a false hope and lends itself to getting into pride. Solomon wisely said, "Pride goes before destruction, and a haughty spirit before a fall" (Proverbs 16:18 NKJV) The Apostle Paul said, "Therefore let him who thinks he stands take heed lest he fall." (1 Corinthians 10:12 NKJV)

"Be sober, be vigilant; because your adversary the devil walks about like a roaring lion, seeking whom he may devour." (1 Peter 5:8 NKJV)

The Apostle Peter understood that distance will create opportunity; therefore, we must be vigilant. Webster's defines the word vigilant as being watchful for possible danger or difficulties. Remember, we have a real adversary who is looking for the weak, the hurting, and those isolated and separating themselves from the Body of Christ. But we have been made stewards, and according to Paul we must be found faithful! We have been given the Great Commission--the mandate to make disciples or even more simply, to "touch as many people as possible!"

Back then, as I perused through the church database, I went to the Senior Associate who oversaw the day-to-day operation of the ministry. I brought to his attention all the people who were missing, some of whom I knew since I had been raised up through that church before coming on staff. As I talked to this man, his eyes filled with tears. I believe that he was sincerely concerned about those people. I also know the background he came from did not place an emphasis on any personal level of ministry. He was not experienced in visiting people, and his primary duties at the ministry were administrative and teaching with a heavy workload. I remember he shook his head, somewhat defeated, and offered no solution about what to do.

A few weeks later, I had the occasion to meet with the Senior Pastor. At this meeting I was given a clear assignment, "Go and touch as many people as possible." Although that church had gone through a split, and in an alarmingly short time, the attendance had dropped in half. I started this assignment with fervor, wanting to honor the command that God had given me through this Pastor.

For 10 1/2 years prior to going into the ministry, I worked for the local water department. When I started out, I was a water meter reader and drove all over the local area, giving me great familiarity with the entire city. I usually read between 500 and 1000 meters per day. As time went on, I was promoted to field collections, and my last position was as an engineering technician on a special project with the department. God used this experience to propel me in the new assignment now given to me. My knowledge of the entire county from north to south made it easy for me to begin to plot out the city and go to the homes of people who previously attended the church. The first 30 days, I went to about 300 homes to get the ball rolling. Then I consistently targeted homes that needed to be reached, going on a regular basis until they were plugged-in to the church. Understand that for my first year, my only responsibility was that of visitation but where we were at the time it was imperative. As a result, the first year I made nearly 3,000 visits to the homes of members and attendees, and the church began to grow.

The following year, additional responsibilities were added to me, and I made approximately 1,800 visits. Over those first two years, we continued to see growth. The day I started we had 296 homes in the church, and within a two-year timeframe of doing visitation, we were back to approximately 600 homes, which meant roughly 1,100 to 1,200 people were in attendance.

I wanted to make sure the door of opportunity would remain open here's how I approached these families. I kept the initial contact very simple, and I asked at every door what their prayer need was. As time went on, I was able to build trust, and the opportunities for real ministry began to open up. For some, it made the difference between them staying involved or leaving the church. Others decided they needed to take their commitment to a new level. The results for first-time visitors being retained was about 44% over a 12 month timeframe. The new convert retention was about 62%, which is highly successful. I truly believe that if more people in the Body of Christ were active in following-up with both the visitors and new converts to a church, that the results would be exceptional. These results came about with just me visiting and a pastoral care secretary calling people.

Look at the increasing church in the book of Acts and you can see that the principle of personal responsibility and follow up was one that everyone in the body participated in. From the beginning, as Peter finished his first sermon, they did not need a class on discipleship, they simply walked it out.

So continuing daily with one accord in the temple, and breaking bread from house to house, they ate their food with gladness and simplicity of heart, praising God and having favor with all the people. And the Lord added to the church daily those who were being saved. (Acts 2:46-47 NKJV)

Here is a picture of the Body of Christ as God wanted it to function and it should be the pattern that we live by. They did not forsake the meeting in the temple for the house meeting. You can see that both were an important part of a thriving, growing Body from the start.

BODY CONSCIOUSNESS

A revelation that really helped me was the fact that we are His body, not just parts! To overcome every challenge, we must start to function just as our physical body does with each member working as God has ordained us to function. If one member hurts, then all hurt with it, and if one rejoices, all rejoice with it.

In the beginning of my ministry, I operated in a partial understanding of this revelation. Believe me, I would have attempted to duplicate myself much more and much sooner had I understood this principle. It does not matter what size your congregation is, you cannot solely have staff ministers as the only ones touching the people. Discipleship must begin to multiply through the church body as a whole, but it starts at the top.

in order to see the value God has placed on people, I had to become body conscious first. Body consciousness was needed for me to get a greater understanding. My efforts increased through those I trained and discipled, keeping the weight of that burden from being too much.

For as we have many members in one body, but all the members do not have the same function, so we, being many, are one body in Christ, and individually members of one another. (Romans 12:4-5 NKJV)

Again, the reality is that no one person can do everything in the local church. The Apostle Paul talked much about the Body of Christ, and in 1 Corinthians, we see how he so wanted them to get the revelation of who they were and what they were capable of.

But now indeed there are many members, yet one body. And the eye cannot say to the hand, "I have no need of you"; nor again the head to the feet, "I have no need of you." No, much rather, those members of the body which seem to be weaker are necessary. And those members of the body which we think to be less honorable, on these we bestow greater honor; and our unpresentable parts have greater modesty, but our presentable parts have no need.

But God composed the body, having given greater honor to that part which lacks it, that there should be no schism in the body, but that the members should have the same care for one another. And if one member suffers, all the members suffer with it; or if one member is honored, all the members rejoice with it. Now you are the Body of Christ, and members individually. (1 Corinthians 12:20-27 NKJV)

Each and every part is important. Look closely at verse 25, Paul said that the "members should have the same care for one another." It specifically points out the members. I am a Pastor's number one advocate when it comes to authority and order in the church. That doesn't mean, however, that the pastor has to do it all. Too many have failed in the ministry because they thought they had to do everything. Many times, there are too many "one-man-shows" and this is destroying the men and women of God.

First and foremost, the Pastor needs to be able to dedicate himself/herself to prayer and the ministry of the Word. If we are to be the glorious church, everyone must become an active part of the body bearing fruit, and seeing the increase that God has ordained for us as the Body of Christ! By the Word of God, we can see that the fivefold ministry gifts are to equip the Body for the work of the ministry for the building up of the Body of Christ. If we are not doing this, we will not move into the fullness of the assignment God has placed on us.

Look back to the garden in Eden when Cain rose against Abel and murdered him. When God confronted Cain, he asked, "Am I my brother's keeper?" When Cain murdered Abel, there was a shirking of the responsibility of personally caring for his brother. As the Body of Christ, we are responsible for each other, and we must take on the mandate to nurture and encourage one another. The excuses of the busyness of the past are no longer acceptable. It is time to awake from sleep and do the work we are assigned to do.

The steps that we will lay out in the following chapters will give some practical guidelines that you can use to get your local body invigorated to go out and care for each other. This will do several things for the church, but the importance of building and strengthening the members of the church cannot be overstated. You can take the guidelines and customize them to the community around you. I have found that, as the Word says, there are diversities of gifts but the same Lord. Let the Holy Spirit give you understanding and guide you as you develop this ministry. He will give you the wisdom to apply this effectively to the church.

I am happy to help guide you through the process. You can email me at rickbarkerministries@gmail.com or visit our website for other resources at: www.rickbarkerministries.com

THE PRACTICAL PLAN

Let's get started with the practical side of visitation and discipleship through personally touching lives. For many in the church, their idea of making disciples is like a course in door-to-door sales. Remember, you are a representative of the Lord Jesus Christ. I have never personally taken the approach to visiting people as being overbearing. To use an old saying, "You never have a second chance to make a first impression." Remember, people will live in the memory of their last (or possibly only) contact with you.

In my years of ministry, I have frequently gone out door to door in the community. When you offer prayer and invite people to services but we should never come off as pushy or insincere. We want the door to remain open and we don't close it by being overbearing or perceived as trying to "sell" them salvation. I will cover various outreach ideas and how-to's in this type of ministry in a later chapter.

When visiting the home of someone who has come to the church or one who has been absent, I generally do not call ahead for my first visit. This may seem rude or unconventional, but I do this with a purpose: it forces me to keep my visit short. You never want to muscle your way in or make the person feel obligated to invite you in. Always ask if they have a minute to talk or not; be sensitive to the Holy Spirit's leading. Learn to read peoples body language of people so that you will leave them with a level of comfort that you can be trusted.

Over the years I have had many experiences. I could probably write a book just on those experiences alone, but I'll only share a few to illustrate my point.

I will never forget this one occasion when I was out with a minister on visitation. When the person we were going to visit answered the door, though not invited, he simply opened the screen door and walked in. It was awkward to say the least. These parents did not attend the church and soon their children stopped coming.

An important key I have learned in life is that what you respect will draw close to you but what you disrespect will go far from you. If you respect those in the home and honor normal boundaries you may well end up winning their favor and winning them to Christ. If I had taken an aggressive approach that would have permanently and irreparably shut the door. There are times God prompts you to be aggressive, but those are exceptions.

INTEGRITY

Some may say this next section is unnecessary, but I believe it must be included. An issue that has permeated the Body of Christ that must be stopped is the issue of "sheep-stealing." I believe that we must never try to build our congregation on another pastor's sheep. Our assignment is to build the Kingdom of God by "preaching the gospel and making disciples."

For we dare not class ourselves or compare ourselves with those who commend themselves. But they, measuring themselves by themselves, and comparing themselves among themselves, are not wise. We, however, will not boast beyond measure, but within the limits of the sphere which God appointed us—a sphere which especially includes you. For we are not overextending ourselves (as though our authority did not extend to you), for it was to you that we came with the gospel of Christ; not boasting of things beyond measure, that is, in other men's labors, but having hope, that as your faith is increased, we shall be greatly enlarged by you in our sphere, to preach the gospel in the regions beyond you, and not to boast in another man's sphere of accomplishment. But "he who glories, let him glory in the Lord." For not he who commends himself is approved, but whom the Lord commends. (2 Corinthians 10:12-18 NKJV)

We are not in a competition, but we are here to complete one another in the ministry. We must only compare ourselves to Jesus and whether or not we are doing what the Head of the church has given us to do. We have a specific duty and responsibility to the members of our church who have been assigned to us. The same is true of members from other congregations--they have a responsibility to those who are assigned to be leaders over them.

We must make a personal commitment that we will not try to draw to our church those who belong to another shepherd. If they are in a church that is not preaching the gospel and equipping the saints for the work of the ministry, maybe then they need to come to our church. But as a rule, this should be the revelation they come to. I have maintained a personal commitment to integrity in building up of the Body of Christ by not recruiting the sheep of another. Transfer growth from other churches is not growth!

God honors our integrity to look to Him for the growth of our church and anything we compromise to get or keep, we will lose. Make the commitment to always walk in sound integrity when it comes to people who attend another church.

> *Most assuredly, I say to you, he who does not enter the sheepfold by the door, but climbs up some other way, the same is a thief and a robber. But he who enters by the door is the shepherd of the sheep. To him the doorkeeper opens, and the sheep hear his voice; and he calls his own sheep by name and leads them out. And when he brings out his own sheep, he goes before them; and the sheep follow him, for they know his voice. Yet they will by no means follow a stranger, but will flee from him, for they do not know the voice of strangers." Jesus used this illustration, but they did not understand the things which He spoke to them. Then Jesus said to them again, "Most assuredly, I say to you, I am the door of the sheep. All who ever came before Me are thieves and robbers, but the sheep did not hear them. I am the door. If anyone enters by Me, he will be saved, and will go in and out and find pasture. The thief does not come except to steal, and to kill, and to destroy. I have come that they may have life, and that they may have it more abundantly. (John 10:1-10 NKJV)*

Jesus said those who come in another way are as thieves and robbers. It should be obvious that we don't want to put ourselves in the same class as satan by stealing what God has assigned to another.

If God tells someone to join your ministry and leave another, make sure that they are not running from correction. Make sure that they have gone to their pastor and have been released. Follow that up by making a personal call to the church to be sure that all is well. We are here to work together, so let's stop allowing the sheep to run from the shepherd and avoid the correction their lives need. You may be thinking, "but if I call their last church they might leave". There may be some who do not want to obey the Word no matter what the cost. Keeping them is not worth the trouble they could cause. If they don't want to submit to even that first phone call, then let them go and pray that they will settle down somewhere.

When I visited someone who has attended one of our services and discover that they are involved in another church in the city, I explain to them that we are here to serve and encourage them to stay with their pastor and serve the vision of that church. From that point on, I don't visit them again. We must refuse to manipulate people to get them into our church.

There have been times a person has said that they may be looking for a change. I encourage them that if God is leading them to leave, they should go to their pastor and get a confirming witness and be properly released from that ministry. I understand there may be some who are coming from a spiritually dead church or a church that is not "Spirit-filled." Encourage people to follow the integrity of the Word in either case. If more churches would do this, we would begin to stem the tide of transfer growth and get busy with winning the lost.

Don't put yourself in a position to influence people to leave a ministry. We are stewards of God's house, not thieves. Remember that you reap what you sow, so if you do not want people trying to manipulate your church members, simply do not sow that. God adds to the church by leading people to Jesus, not by manipulation.

When a church is going through strife or rebellion, sometimes pastors see themselves as saviors of the body. Too often they capitalize on the strife and challenges of fellow ministers. We must be sure we are never party to this--that type of growth will never last. When a church and its leader are going through an attack, let's stand with them by undergirding them in prayer and supporting them by being a friend.

If we are busy fulfilling scripture, then we need not influence people who are assigned to another pastor. There are enough people for every church in all of our cities. If we reached every person for Christ, every church would be filled to capacity, and the job would still not be complete. Satan is the only one who wants to cause strife and division, and this must cease in the Body of Christ.

Behold, how good and how pleasant it is for brethren to dwell together in unity! It is like the precious oil upon the head, running down on the beard, The beard of Aaron, Running down on the edge of his garments. It is like the dew of Hermon, descending upon the mountains of Zion; For there the LORD commanded the blessing—Life forevermore. (Psalm 133:1-3 NKJV)

If we will dwell together in our cities in the unity of the faith, with our brothers and sisters in Christ, we will see a release of the anointing of God that we've never seen before. It will be the release of the former and latter rain of the Holy Ghost upon the Church. (Joel 2:23 NKJV)

CONSISTENCY

Another key to a successful visitation and discipleship ministry is that of consistency. Let's not be like the guy who heard about tithing and only did it for two weeks. He stopped because he didn't get a promotion at work and his debt was not cancelled.

When I make these calls, my goal is not to get all the results in one visit. I generally make several short visits to a home to build trust and to establish a relationship with people. Do you let just anybody into your home when they show up? I would dare say the answer is no. Put yourself in the shoes of another and this will help you see from their perspective. Never approach a door like a salesman! I do not believe would Jesus come off like an arrogant salesman and neither should we.

Once, I was with a minister who had the salesman approach. It made those we visited very uncomfortable. We cannot be effective by trying to "sell them" on the church. Just be real, be sincere. Live out the principles of Jesus and let God add to the church by bringing conviction into the lives of those you touch. There have been homes I have visited for years because I was sensitive to what God was doing.

Another benefit of personal visitation is how it helps members whose spouses don't attend the church. By the persoan touch of a visit, I have seen unbelieving spouses start attending church and getting saved.

Let me share some testimonies. A family in our city lost their son in a tragic hit and run accident. Their daughter had attended our church for many years. When we got the news of this terrible loss, a group of us from the church were present and available to that family throughout the funeral and days that followed. In the weeks and years after that, we walked with them through some tough places. This family was not in church or serving God prior to this tragedy, but through the consistency of care and personal visitation they are serving God today. I believe that if we were just there to conduct a funeral service that we would not have had the same results. Romans 2:4 tells us, "It is the goodness of God that leads sinners to repent."

Another situation included a wife who began to attend and even got saved. The husband didn't attend regularly but supported his children and wife's involvement. His sister and mother had been faithful members of the church for some time. I visited the home and one day the husband asked me to stop coming by unannounced. I respected that boundary and didn't harbor an offense. I would still call them on the phone periodically to check on them, and every time he would say it was not a good time to visit. Even if a person asks you to stop visiting, you never stop caring. We know that God can, and often does, change boundaries. Consistent personal care opened the door to this man's heart. He is now regularly attending a local church and has for many years. He's gone through discipleship training and is a very committed part of the ministry. Consistent care is what drew him and is keeping him. Over the years, I have walked him and his family through the loss of a dear uncle, financial hardship, and other tough places, and he has pressed through each one and continues to serve today.

I could tell you story after story where God has used visitation ministry to see great miracles take place in people's lives. I have seen people healed of cancer, seen others receive financial miracles, and some have been filled with the Spirit. Most importantly others have made a commitment to Jesus.

Once again, the key is that it is not what you did once or do occasionally that will make the difference, but what you are doing on a continual basis. Galatians 6:9 says, "Don't grow weary in well doing for in due season you reap if you don't give up." There is a due season for everything but until we are consistent in fulfilling the Word in this area, we will see the lasting results of adding to the church.

If we make a commitment to make visitations a part of our lives and ministry, there will be results like nothing we have done before to build a work that will last.

SETTING THE STANDARD

As we press forward with the assignment God has given, He will stir the hearts of people more and more to reach the lost. Start where you are; be patient and be consistent. I want to make some suggestions that may stir your heart to the Father's plan.

First, make sure that you manage your time to allow you to go on some visits (it is important that you have those who come alongside to help). If you are the pastor of your congregation, people will move in the direction that you are going. However, make sure to protect your time with God in study and preparation. It is vital that you stay full of God!

It is a good idea that you make your leaders your first priority in visitation. When you focus on your leaders making them a priority it sets the standard for them. Getting into the home is one of the key ways that you will truly find out where your leaders need help in focusing on personal excellence. If they are not walking in personal excellence at home, it will show at some point in their responsibilities in church. If you arrive to a home that has dishes piled high, weeds taking over, paint chipping and chaos abounding, they may need to take some time out so that they can focus on the home front. although this is just an example, it's a sample of how we can help them see our heart: that their personal well-being is our highest priority. You need a team that is free of distraction and placing a personal emphasis on them will also build their confidence in your leadership.

When you visit the home of a leader you may discover why you don't see the spouse but once a week. If this is the case don't be afraid to begin to help. Remember, what you compromise to keep you will lose. It will be a whole lot worse later if you ignore a problem you discover. A leader whose homes or marriages are out of sorts are not in the best place to lead at the moment and that's okay. If you help them get to a place where they can deal with their weakness, the kingdom will be rewarded in the strength of your leadership base.

Another key is the stewardship of your time. If someone needs counsel when you visit with them, keep that time to about one hour. Whatever the need is, it will not likely be resolved in one sitting. Another time can be set up that will allow you the time to better meet their needs.

An important key to disciple your leaders, invest in them and they will be your greatest asset in building the church. Some situations may dictate that you spend more time in discipleship but just be cognizant of boundaries when helping people. I have found that in churches that minister the uncompromised Word of God, there is usually little need for individual counsel if true discipleship is taking place. Be sensitive of your time and theirs. There will likely be situations, when the enemy will attempt to steal your time helping insincere people who are not interested in applying God's Word to their life. Discern that quickly and move on.

A great way to multiply your efforts is through mentorship and training. To create an environment of discipleship is the responsibility of all in the church. If you build from your leadership core outward, though slow, it will eventually have an exponential affect.

And He Himself gave some to be apostles, some prophets, some evangelists, and some pastors and teachers, for the equipping of the saints for the work of ministry, for the edifying of the Body of Christ. (Ephesians 4:11-12 NKJV)

God never intended for the pastor to do ministry alone. We must train and mentor others to do the work of the ministry and alongside us. Now, let's focus on who is qualified for our mentorship? Let's look to scripture and see how God used Moses' father-in-law to give him wisdom on this matter.

So, the Lord said to Moses: "Gather to Me seventy men of the elders of Israel, whom you know to be the elders of the people and officers over them; bring them to the tabernacle of meeting, that they may stand there with you. Then I will come down and talk with you there. I will take of the Spirit that is upon you and will put the same upon them; and they shall bear burden of the people with you, that you may not bear it yourself alone. (Numbers 11:16-17 NKJV)

Now the seventy were for the whole body of the children of Israel. They helped ease the load for Moses. Like Moses, you need to find someone who has the anointing to help you.

QUALITIES & QUALIFICATIONS OF ASSISTANTS

Statistically, it is said that one minister can take care of about 150-200 people. Though that may be, how many did Jesus actually invest personally in? He appointed the twelve apostles but dedicated a lot of time to Peter, James, and John.

Find people whose hearts are to help you build the vision God gave for your church. Find a person who has already proven they are faithful. Find someone who will work with very little prompting or supervision. Although there needs to be accountability find someone you don't need to babysit or always have to prod to do the will of God. I started visitation long before I became a fulltime minister and was very involved in helping with whatever was needed. Paul helped us with written guidelines that allow us to see who is qualified.

This is a faithful saying: If a man desires the position of a bishop, he desires a good work. A bishop then must be blameless, the husband of one wife, temperate, sober-minded, of good behavior, hospitable, able to teach; not given to wine, not violent, not greedy for money, but gentle, not quarrelsome, not covetous; one who rules his own house well, having his children in submission with all reverence (for if a man does not know how to rule his own house, how will he take care of the church of God?); not a novice, lest being puffed up with pride he fall into the same condemnation as the devil. Moreover, he must have a good testimony among those who are outside, lest he fall into reproach and the snare of the devil. Likewise, deacons must be reverent, not double-tongued, not given to much wine, not greedy for money, holding the mystery of the faith with a pure conscience. But let these also first be tested; then let them serve as deacons, being found blameless. Likewise, their wives must be reverent, not slanderers, temperate, faithful in all things. Let deacons be the husbands of one wife, ruling their children and their own houses well. For those who have served well as deacons obtain for themselves a good standing and great boldness in the faith which is in Christ Jesus. (1 Timothy 3:1-13 NKJV)

Here the word bishop here is episkopos meaning a superintendent, Christian officer in charge of a church or lay minister, a public servant. Paul told Timothy that they must be blameless, not perfect but blameless, above reproach. If perfection were part of the qualifications, no one would be able to qualify for the ministry. Our lives become blameless as we walk before God and allow Him to deal with the issues of our character.

Paul also dealt with the issue of deacons. This is the word diakonos, meaning to run errands, an attendant, a waiter at a table or in other menial duties. This does not mean they are less important, but there are some who love to serve in the practical aspects of life and ministry. Look for those who are satisfied doing whatever God assigns them to do and are not looking for recognition. The person helping you needs to be one who does not have a personal agenda. They must be a person of integrity, a person who will bring honor to your church and ministry. You need a team who will stick with you through thick and thin. Realize that God will bring promotion to the faithful. If one will be faithful with what is in their hands--root down and determine to keep the right focus--God will bring the promotion that their life has qualified them for.

VISITATION TEAMS

An important way of achieving effective outreach and follow-up ministry is by developing teams. I suggest that the teams consist of a minimum of two people: a married couple, two women or two men. If a person has their life properly prioritized, loves the Lord, and allows themselves to be taught, they can do this. You never know who will shine through and show that they are qualified and called to be a minister. Experientially, it is far more fruitful to raise up and personally disciple and mentor a minister than try to send them off to a Bible College. If you have been around the ministry at all, as is often the case is that you send good dedicated servants to Bible College and few will ever return to your ministry.

> *Now in those days, when the number of the disciples was multiplying, there arose a complaint against the Hebrews by the Hellenists, because their widows were neglected in the daily distribution. Then the twelve summoned the multitude of the disciples and said, "It is not desirable that we should leave the word of God and serve tables. Therefore, brethren, seek out from among you seven men of good reputation, full of the Holy Spirit and wisdom, whom we may appoint over this business; but we will give ourselves continually to prayer and to the ministry of the word." And the saying pleased the whole multitude. And they chose Stephen, a man full of faith and the Holy Spirit, and Philip, Prochorus, Nicanor, Timon, Parmenas, and Nicolas, a proselyte from Antioch, whom they set before the apostles; and when they had prayed, they laid hands on them. Then the word of God spread, and the number of the disciples multiplied greatly in Jerusalem, and a great many of the priests were obedient to the faith. (Acts 6:1-7 NKJV)*

Out of those chosen, Stephen and Philip increased in the anointing because of their faithfulness and did mighty exploits in Jesus' name. The result was that the church increased and multiplied. This was merely the beginning. The Apostles began by setting the example for the Body to follow. The book of Acts states they continued steadfastly in the doctrine, fellowship, breaking of bread and praying of prayers. (Acts 2:42 NKJV) In Acts 11, after Stephen was murdered the church scattered, but it increases as the people went out preaching the Gospel.

Now those who were scattered after the persecution that arose over Stephen traveled as far as Phoenicia, Cyprus, and Antioch, preaching the word to no one but the Jews only. But some of them were men from Cyprus and Cyrene, who, when they had come to Antioch, spoke to the Hellenists, preaching the Lord Jesus. And the hand of the Lord was with them, and a great number believed and turned to the Lord. Then news of these things came to the ears of the church in Jerusalem, and they sent out Barnabas to go as far as Antioch. When he came and had seen the grace of God, he was glad, and encouraged them all that with purpose of heart they should continue with the Lord. For he was a good man, full of the Holy Spirit and of faith. And a great many people were added to the Lord. (Acts 11:19-24 NKJV)

It is time for us to take the lid off the box the church is in and allow God to do as He did in the book of Acts--increasing and multiplying the Body of Christ. As we fulfill the ministry we have been given and equip the saints we serve, we will see unity, growth, and the supernatural take place more and more.

NEVER ROUTINE

Don't let reaching people become just a process. If you lose sight that this is all about touching people and fulfilling God's purpose, you can abd will get discouraged. Remember, some plant, some water, God gives the increase! Don't let what you see or don't see dictate how effective you think you are being in the ministry. Look at the long-term and see the results in terms of seedtime and harvest. Go expecting results! Your perspective will affect your results. Don't just focus on the natural or that which is seen.

Your focus will always affect what God is able to do through your efforts. Jesus kept going in His ministry even though He knew that one of His disciples would betray Him. Some you touch may turn on you--it happened to Jesus, it has happened to me, and it will probably happen to you. These are a small percentage of the people we touch and yet they often get the most attention. Don't lose site of the miracles, breakthroughs, and testimonies of lives touched and changed as you go out and let God work through you. Don't forget they are God's and not yours anyway. We are stewards, not owners.

> *And let us not grow weary while doing good, for in due season we shall reap if we do not lose heart.10 Therefore, as we have opportunity, let us do good to all, especially to those who are of the household of faith. (Galatians 6:9-10 NKJV)*

God rewards the faithful, continual work of His leaders and the Body of Christ. Never, never, never quit or give up!

7

THE HOW TO'S

This section will give you the necessary tools for winning the lost and making true disciples of the Lord Jesus Christ! These include repentance, deliverance, praying for the sick, and walking in your authority over every power of the enemy. I will endeavor to cover most common ministry needs you will find while out with people.

It is important, first and foremost, that we never preach a gospel that has no repentance. It is equally important that we share with people that they are not coming to Santa God, or to meet their laundry list of needs, wants and desires.

We are not coming to a God merely of love, who just wants to make our lives better, help us lose unwanted weight, make our teeth brighter or breath fresher or make our marriage perfect. We never want people to get the impression that, like so much of our world today, this is some kind of quick fix formula.

We must help people understand that God is Holy and just and His standard is perfection. I heard one minister use the illustration of two people who are taking a flight. The first is given a parachute when he boarded the plane and told if he puts on the parachute, he will have a better flight. The man really does not see how this could make his flight better but reluctantly complies with the request. Immediately, he notices the weight and discomfort that the parachute gives him but keeps it on and tries to sit down. When he does, he then notices, in addition to the weight, that he cannot sit correctly further adding to his discomfort. Then, to top it all off, the other passengers begin pointing, laughing, and making fun of him. Out of frustration and embarrassment he stands up and throws the chute to the ground declaring, "I was lied to! This didn't make my flight better; it only made it miserable!"

The second man who received his chute was told, "Sir, put this parachute on because when we reach 20,000 feet you will be required to jump from the plane." Well, with this information, the man is so grateful and realizes that without the chute he is doomed and even though it is heavy and a bit uncomfortable he hardly notices it because of his gratitude to the flight attendant for saving his life.

Oftentimes, those who have received the gospel have been told, "come to Jesus, He will make your life better." But in time, as the weight and pressure of walking a different lifestyle becomes a reality, they will give up and quit. When leading people to Jesus let us not be guilty of giving them the person of Jesus without bringing them to know the principles of Jesus.

An excellent way of effectively sharing the gospel is by taking a person first to the point of the Ten Commandments. The Apostle Paul said, "I would have not known sin except through the law" (Romans 7:7).

Let's start with the first commandment, "you shall have no other gods before me." A god can be anyone or anything you put ahead of your relationship with God in order of importance in life. Relationships with a member of the opposite sex or parents or children, perhaps. Hobbies or disproportionate career choices and the list could go on. Most people would have to admit that when it comes to that standard, we have all missed it at some point regarding placing people or things ahead of God.

He who loves father or mother more than Me is not worthy of Me. And he who loves son or daughter more than Me is not worthy of Me. And he who does not take his cross and follow after Me is not worthy of Me. He who finds his life will lose it, and he who loses his life for My sake will find it. (Matthew 10:37-39 NKJV)

The second commandment says that you shall not create any idols. Many believe that a "good" God would never send a good person to hell. Well, they are right because they have created an image of God in their mind that does not match the God of the bible and have created an idol in their mind. We are created in His image and likeness, and we must only formulate the true image of God through what His Word says and not through our opinion. This is what the Pharisees and Sadducees did and it made them guilty of all. Jesus called them a bunch of snakes. They had built in their mind an image of the Savior that did not fit that of Jesus. They created an idol in their mind of how the Messiah would look.

The third commandment says that we should not take God's name in vain. Well, you can ask the person you are witnessing to, "Have you ever used Gods name in the midst of cursing?" For example, uttering "Jesus Christ" out of frustration and not because you were calling on Him for help.

For whoever shall keep the whole law, and yet stumble in one point, he is guilty of all. (James 2:10 NKJV)

As you continue to go point to point from commandment to commandment, allow the Holy Spirit to help drive the conviction deep into the heart of the person.

The fourth commandment- to keep the Sabbath Holy- really could get them. I remember I used to be out there on Saturday night partying with the crowd and the last thing I wanted to do come Sunday was set aside time to worship God. And I know some may read this who worship on Saturday and believe that is the only time we should worship. I can respect your opinion on that but the real principle that we must keep here is that every day is a day that must be set aside to worship Him. Even the Apostle Paul, in his letter to the Galatians, dealt with this issue.

But now after you have known God, or rather are known by God, how is it that you turn again to the weak and beggarly elements, to which you desire again to be in bondage? You observe days and months and seasons and years. I am afraid for you, lest I have labored for you in vain. (Galatians 4:9-11 NKJV)

Don't allow there to be a loss of focus here arguing over what the Sabbath is. Stay on task with your witness, the bottom line is to regularly set aside a day for God.

Commandment number five, "Honor your father and mother." In this day and age, we see much in the way of disrespect regarding mother and father. God did not qualify this command by saying honor them if . . . He simply said, "Honor your father and mother."

What about the love you have or express toward others? The world today has boiled down the word love to mean so little.

But according to God the type of love we need to walk in when it comes to honoring others is agape. This is the love that God expressed toward us through the sacrifice of His Son, Jesus. Agape does not base its response on what another has done but gives and loves without regard to whether or not the one for whom the love is expressed deserves it or not.

I know that it seems easier to say, "my parents hurt me, therefore I don't have to honor them". But ask this question-do you want that same type of response given to you by your children? One day, the reality sinks in for all of us that there is no perfect human parent. Ephesians 6:1 says, that to honor father and mother comes with a promise for things to be well with you and that you may live long on the earth!

You know with all the talk about banning guns today, this is a sensitive topic, but I will not avoid its discussion. God said, do not murder! Not many of us will say we have murdered anyone, I am sure. But look at what the New Testament says about murder. Jesus said if you are angry with your brother without a cause you are in danger of judgment. The Apostle John also addressed this, "Anyone who hates his brother is a murderer, and you know that no murderer has eternal life in him." (1 John 3:15 NIV)

You can make laws, ban guns, and make every effort to stop the tragedy we see unfold all too often. Nevertheless, the only way to stop the madness of murder is to deal with the heart! If your heart is filled with hate, you have already murdered in your heart! Today, it seems that spills over into the natural world far too easily. When we help bring life, forgiveness, and healing to hearts, we will see a difference made in our sphere of influence.

Do not commit adultery, yet Jesus took this on and said if you look at a woman to lust after her in your heart, you have already committed adultery in your heart (Matthew 5:27-28 NKJV). We have been called to live by a higher standard than the law. Each point to the Ten Commandments helps you realize more and more that you can never attain righteousness with God.

"Do not steal!" As you lead the discussion you can take this person to a place of admission that we have all stolen something at some time. I have only had one person tell me they have not stolen even a little thing ever. Most people understand that merely taking a pen from the office is technically theft but, you know, if you run up against this response, don't get stuck. It's far easier to give them a high five and move on.

Do not lie. Whoa, here is one that we certainly all have missed a time or two.

Finally, do not covet. In other words, have you ever wanted something that belonged to someone else? Then you missed it here, also.

Now remember the Apostle Paul on several occasions used the law to bring people to the point of realization that we all need a Savior. Galatians 3:24, "Therefore the law was our tutor to bring us to Christ, that we might be justified by faith."

The point of using the law as our basis is not to leave people in the place of bondage and oppression, but to get them to the place of answering the question. "How can I ever make it to heaven then?" The answer is simply this- you can't! But God sent someone to pay the price of the standard of perfection so that you could gain right standing before Him.

Therefore, if anyone is in Christ, he is a new creation; old things have passed away; behold, all things have become new. Now all things are of God, who has reconciled us to Himself through Jesus Christ, and has given us the ministry of reconciliation, that is, that God was in Christ reconciling the world to Himself, not imputing their trespasses to them, and has committed to us the word of reconciliation. (2 Corinthians 5:17-19 NKJV)

Jesus told Nicodemus in John, chapter 3, that unless you are born-again you would not see the Kingdom of God. You must be born of water and of the Spirit. When a person is born into the world, they are born of water but to be born of the Spirit is a choice; it comes by faith in Christ Jesus.

But what does it say? "The word is near you, in your mouth and in your heart" (that is, the word of faith which we preach): that if you confess with your mouth the Lord Jesus and believe in your heart that God has raised Him from the dead, you will be saved. For with the heart one believes unto righteousness, and with the mouth confession is made unto salvation. (Romans 10:8-11 NKJV)

We have so many promises from the word declaring what Christ did for us in His death, burial and resurrection. He redeemed us from the curse of the law according to Galatians 3:13. Glory to God when we take people to that place of intimacy with the Father and to the place of reality, whereby they can be made perfect in Christ. Then, we will begin to transform the world around us one person at a time.

The book of Philippians says that Jesus walked in obedience to the point of death. This should be the attitude of our heart as we go out, not seeking our own glory but the glory of God. Jesus never said that following His command would be convenient or easy. Examine what He did and how He walked.

Your attitude should be the same as that of Christ Jesus: Who, being in very nature God, did not consider equality with God something to be grasped, but made himself nothing, taking the very nature of a servant, being made in human likeness. And being found in appearance as a man, he humbled himself and became obedient to death- even death on a cross! Therefore, God exalted him to the highest place and gave him the name that is above every name, that at the name of Jesus every knee should bow, in heaven and on earth and under the earth, and every tongue confess that Jesus Christ is Lord, to the glory of God the Father. (Philippians 2:5-11 NIV)

The road that we must walk is a road that is not walked down carelessly or with little regard or focus on others. Until the Body of Christ is living for others, we are not really living at all.

Enter by the narrow gate; for wide is the gate and broad is the way that leads to destruction, and there are many who go in by it. Because narrow is the gate and difficult is the way which leads to life, and there are few who find it. (Matthew 7:13-14 NKJV)

To walk in the narrow place, you must focus, or you will miss it every time. In life, it's easy to go along with the crowd. The problem is that path brings nothing but destruction into our lives. We don't want to portray a false gospel by painting an unrealistic picture that there will never be another problem or challenge in the life of those who give their lives to Jesus. But we must let them know that we are partners with them to stand and use the authority of the Word to overcome every issue the enemy could throw their way. The devil has nothing new he can throw at us, every scheme that he has is just an old, worn-out attempt to cause destruction in the lives of God's people.

THE BAPTISM IN THE HOLY SPIRIT

After leading a person into a relationship with Jesus it is important that they get all that God has for them. Every tool and every resource are designed to help them walk in victory. Other than the principle of giving and receiving, the Baptism of the Holy Spirit is one of the most misunderstood subjects that the devil has used to bring confusion into the Body of Christ. After you lead a person to the Lord you will need to discern as to whether or not the time is right for them to receive the Baptism in the Holy Spirit. Some, like myself, grew up with a very great lack of understanding as to the scriptural benefits of this gift! If ready, get them resources and give them scriptures that will help them see that this experience is for them.

You will also find many who have served the Lord for many years and never received the Baptism in the Holy Spirit. It was that way for me, I grew up where that was not even a part of our belief system. But God brought me to a church that believed in speaking in tongues. My experience was supernatural! For several weeks after I started to attend this church, I did not hear people around me praying in tongues. In Acts 2, we see an example of what happened to me, those who heard them heard them speaking in the language in which they were born. It was not until I had read mini books like Kenneth Hagin's Why Tongues, that I began to see through the word that the baptism in the Holy Spirit was an experience I could have. In fact, I remember the first time I even heard someone speak in tongues was when I was listening to a radio broadcast of a church service.

The hungrier I became, the more I experienced frustration because I did not have a full understanding of how to receive. I prayed the prayers in the books I read and got nothing. I cried out to God for help and He heard and answered my prayer by sending someone in the church to help me with receiving. As they walked me through the scriptures, I began to see that receiving this gift was the same as receiving the righteousness of God, by faith! The moment this person laid hands on me, I received and spoke in other tongues.

After I received the Baptism in the Holy Spirit, I remember the word of God coming to life so much more than it had previously. God totally brought transformation into me with this experience. It is my prayer, as you share with others, that God uses you in the same powerful way.

Here are some scriptures that you can use to lead a person in the Baptism in the Holy Spirit. First, start at the beginning of Acts chapter 1, with the instruction that Jesus gave. He told them to wait in Jerusalem until they received the promise of the Father. This was the one and only time in scripture that we see a command to wait to receive this gift. In Acts 2, on the day of Pentecost, there were 120 in the upper room when the sound like a rushing mighty wind came in and filled the place and each one spoke with tongues. Such was the experience that they spilled out into the street. (Acts 2:5-12 NKJV)

Such was the sight that they were really confused as to what this meant and immediately Peter has the opportunity and preaches his first sermon. It was the beginning of the prophecy Joel shared about the last days. As Peter declares to them Jesus as the Savior, the conviction of the Holy Spirit comes and they are born-again and though Acts 2 does not expressly say that they spoke with tongues, I believe we can see from other scripture that they must have. We know from the story of Cornelius in Acts 10; they absolutely spoke with tongues.

And those of the circumcision who believed were astonished, as many as came with Peter, because the gift of the Holy Spirit had been poured out on the Gentiles also. (Acts 10:45 NKJV)

If they who were of the circumcision had not received, they would not have been astonished. We can also look at the pattern of the scripture in the record of Acts 11 when the Holy Spirit touched the lives of those who had believed in Jesus.

Now when the apostles who were at Jerusalem heard that Samaria had received the word of God, they sent Peter and

John to them, who, when they had come down, prayed for them that they might receive the Holy Spirit. For as yet He had fallen upon none of them. They had only been baptized in the name of the Lord Jesus. Then they laid hands on them, and they received the Holy Spirit. (Acts 8:14-17 NKJV)

They received without waiting, without praying and crying out to God. Simply put, Peter and John laid hands on them and they received. We will never fail by following the pattern of the word.

Someone may ask why it's such a big deal to pray in other tongues. In fact, I am certain you will face this question. Romans 8:26, "For we do not know what we should pray for as we ought." I remember one time needing to pray over a situation before receiving the baptism in the Holy Spirit. This was potentially a life and death matter! Imagine, I only knew how to pray in my understanding and for days I did so. Imagine the confidence I would have had if I had been tapped into the flow of the Spirit by praying in tongues! First Corinthians 14:4 says, "He who speaks in a tongue edifies himself." God had such mercy on me because I did not have much understanding but, I was all in! The sooner we can get people to the place of receiving through a discipleship environment the better.

Anyone who is a believer can minister the Baptism in the Holy Spirit and God will honor your faith. After Saul of Tarsus saw Jesus on the road to Damascus, God did not send him the big-name evangelist or the Apostle Peter, He sent Ananias. (Acts 9:10-18 NKJV) Ananias was someone just like any member of any church in the world today who simply obeyed the instruction of the Lord. But if someone hadn't responded, we might be missing a good portion of the bible today. This isn't the only time God used someone other than a five-fold minister to get the work of the ministry accomplished.

In Acts 6, among those chosen, I want to note Stephen who was full of faith and preached the gospel to his dying breath. Then there is Phillip, whose faithfulness brought him into the five-fold. But they both started by just being faithful with the God given assignment of serving widows in the distribution of food.

In Acts 19:1-6, The Apostle Paul came upon some disciples at Corinth and he asked them if they had received the Holy Spirit since they believed. As it turned out, they had not even been born-again. We must use the word of God to get people to the place of faith and receiving. This is not by natural understanding but it is spiritually discerned and received. If you end up dealing with someone who is a thinker, you are really going to have to get them to a place that they are not trying to reason or rationalize all that is going on. If they try to process it by natural thinking, they will not receive.

But God has revealed them to us through His Spirit. For the Spirit searches all things, yes, the deep things of God. For what man knows the things of a man except the spirit of the man which is in him? Even so no one knows the things of God except the Spirit of God. Now we have received, not the spirit of the world, but the Spirit who is from God, that we might know the things that have been freely given to us by God. These things we also speak, not in words which man's wisdom teaches but which the Holy Spirit teaches, comparing spiritual things with spiritual. But the natural man does not receive the things of the Spirit of God, for they are foolishness to him; nor can he know them, because they are spiritually discerned. (1 Corinthians 2:10-14 NKJV)

God will only reveal spiritual revelation to us through His Spirit, not to our mind, but to our spirit. It is impossible for the natural man to receive these things; they are foolish to the natural mind. Romans 10:17 says, "Faith comes by hearing". Share the Word, not just your experience, and you will have success every time. If they choose not to receive, don't give up. Remember that some plant, some water but God will bring the increase.

MINISTERING HEALING

I have had many occasions to minister healing to both the saved and unsaved alike. Regardless of where God has taken me and who is our audience, we must always be instant in and out of season. I have had the wonderful opportunity to be used by God in healing as I just share the word in faith. In the Great Commission we have been given, the Word declares that the believer will lay hands on the sick. (Mark 16:15-18 NKJV)

It does not say that the Apostle, Prophet, Pastor, Teacher or Evangelist will lay hands on the sick but that these signs will follow those who believe. As I have watched others get out and walk in obedience to this word, it is amazing to see how God honors their faith to His word by moving mightily when they pray. I would encourage you to use the scriptures to establish God's will more so than just the testimony of someone who was healed of cancer. I am not saying that sharing a testimony isn't powerful, I am merely encouraging you to use the Word as the foundation of that platform.

With some people, you may have to get them to realize that Jesus made them worthy to receive the promise of healing. One of the greatest hindrances to healing is that a person thinks, somehow, that they have to measure up and qualify for God to heal them. A great scripture to use is 2 Corinthians 5:21, "He made Him who knew no sin to be sin for us that we might be made the righteousness of God in Him." This establishes to them that the price of worthiness was paid on the cross. Acts 10:34 says, "God is no respecter of persons," what He has done for anyone throughout time ever, He will do for you!

HEALING SCRIPTURES

Surely, He has borne our griefs and carried our sorrows; Yet we esteemed Him stricken, Smitten by God, and afflicted. But He was wounded for our transgressions, He was bruised for our iniquities; The chastisement for our peace was upon Him, And by His stripes we are healed. (Isaiah 53:4-5 NKJV)

He sent His word and healed them, and delivered them from their destructions. (Psalm 107:20 NKJV)

Christ has redeemed us from the curse of the law, having become a curse for us (for it is written, "Cursed is everyone who hangs on a tree", that the blessing of Abraham might come upon the Gentiles in Christ Jesus, that we might receive the promise of the Spirit through faith. (Galatians 3:13-14 NKJV)

For to this you were called, because Christ also suffered for us, leaving us an example, that you should follow His steps: "Who committed no sin, Nor was deceit found in His mouth"; who, when He was reviled, did not revile in return; when He suffered, He did not threaten, but committed Himself to Him who judges righteously; who Himself bore our sins in His own body on the tree, that we, having died to sins, might live for righteousness—by whose stripes you were healed. (1 Peter 2:21-24 NKJV)

These are some key scriptures I use when ministering healing. This is not an exhaustive list but you can use this as a tool to build the faith of those who are in need of healing.

OPERATING IN THE GIFTS

It is important as you go out to minister to others that you always be open to the Holy Spirit's leading in the use of the gifts God has given you. The Apostle Paul encouraged the Body of Christ to be functional in its assigned place.

> *For I say, through the grace given to me, to everyone who is among you, not to think of himself more highly than he ought to think, but to think soberly, as God has dealt to each one a measure of faith. For as we have many members in one body, but all the members do not have the same function, so we, being many, are one body in Christ, and individually members of one another. Having then gifts differing according to the grace that is given to us, let us use them: if prophecy, let us prophesy in proportion to our faith; or ministry, let us use it in our ministering; he who teaches, in teaching; he who exhorts, in exhortation; he who gives, with liberality; he who leads, with diligence; he who shows mercy, with cheerfulness. (Romans 12:3-8 NKJV)*

As God has gifted you, use that gift for His glory as you go out fulfilling the assignment, He has given to all the Body of Christ to win the lost. When things start happening through your obedience to the Word, just remember who it is that has bestowed the gift you possess. Too often I have watched people start to be used of God and get the wrong impression that it was because of them that the miracles happened. Keep a constant intimacy with God so that you will keep the right perspective.

Now, I want to cover the biblical principle of the nine gifts of the spirit. The utterance, revelation and power gifts will often manifest as you go out and follow the command of Jesus to preach the gospel to every creature.

> *There are diversities of gifts, but the same Spirit. There are differences of ministries, but the same Lord. And there are diversities of activities, but it is the same God who works all in all. But the manifestation of the Spirit is given to each one for the profit of all: for to one is given the word of wisdom*

through the Spirit, to another the word of knowledge through the same Spirit, to another faith by the same Spirit, to another gifts of healings by the same Spirit, to another the working of miracles, to another prophecy, to another discerning of spirits, to another different kinds of tongues, to another the interpretation of tongues. But one and the same Spirit works all these things, distributing to each one individually as He wills. (1 Corinthians 12:4-11 NKJV)

I want to point you to a resource that is an excellent, deep teaching about these gifts. Brother Kenneth E. Hagin, "The Holy Spirit and His Gifts". This is one of the most extensive teachings on this subjects and I want to encourage you to take full advantage of what God has given us through Brother Hagin.

THE UTTERANCE GIFTS

When out ministering with people, do not be surprised if you receive a prophetic word for someone to whom you are ministering. With that said, I want to encourage you to do so with balance. I have seen many people hurt by those who abuse or misuse a word of prophecy and cause people to stumble. Falling in the category of the utterance gifts, it can come directly or with a tongue and interpretation equaling a prophecy. Prophecy is a message that is directly from the heart of God and is designed to build up the person. But he who prophesies speaks edification and exhortation and comfort to men (1 Corinthians 14:3).

Therefore, this gift, in its proper use and setting lends itself to the building up of the Body of Christ. Prophecy is not fortune telling or mind reading and has nothing to do with the New Age movement. Prophecy is also not God telling on someone! Make sure that what you speak is coming from God and not your opinion about something you heard about a person or situation. This is a very holy thing and we must not contaminate it with human knowledge. I have seen people speak things that absolutely were not from God but from their own mind and were works of the flesh.

THE REVELATION GIFTS

I have had the experience, as I was out ministering to people, when God would give me a word of wisdom or word of knowledge or, at times, I have operated in the discerning of spirits. Let's cover each one of these individually because they could get you into some really awkward positions if you don't really understand them.

The word of knowledge is when you know the facts about a thing that it is not humanly impossible for you to have known. In other words, no person revealed the facts to you. I have had this happen many times where I will be out and God will reveal to me something that has taken place. The next step to this is asking God for wisdom on what to do with that information. Sometimes you pray and other times you need to act. Knowing the difference will save you a lot of trouble in carrying out the great commission.

The word of wisdom is information concerning future events. When you start dealing with people, it is important to know how to deal with some of the things you will encounter. There are times people will want to know, from the Word, how to take care of the basic issues of life. If you haven't dealt with it before, God can and will help you assist them by giving you the answers- you can and must believe Him for that. Experience for yourself the tremendous growth, as a result of being open to the word and wisdom, that only God can give.

The discerning of spirits is one that can really get you into some trouble. Many have recognized it as the "gift" of discernment, which is not, in actuality, a gift but the result of wisdom growing in your life. (Proverbs 2:1-9 NKJV) The discerning of spirits is not the gift of judgment about someone's motives or intentions. The discerning of spirits is the ability to discern the nature of a spirit behind a situation as to whether it is the Holy Spirit, a demon, or the human spirit.

I remember a time before I was in the full-time ministry, I was working for the county water department and a customer came in, which was entirely commonplace. As I began to help this person and explain to them they needed a few other items, this guy begins to beat himself in the head with his fist. Well, you have two directions you could go here, get into fear or get the mind of God. I chose the latter and I immediately knew in my spirit this guy was not just dealing with a mental issue. There was an evil spirit in this man and so I quietly reached across the desk and said, "satan, I bind you in Jesus' name." I certainly did not cause a scene (though the customer was!) and though I was not overtly vocal about it, the man immediately calmed down and we were able to complete our business. Without the discerning of spirits in operation I could have gotten in fear or tried to do something I should not have done in that situation. Remember this, however, that these gifts operate as the Spirit of God wills and He will give you what you need when you need it.

THE POWER GIFTS

The gift of faith, gifts of healings and working of miracles oftentimes work together. The gift of faith is not another kind of faith that one person would have over another. Rather, the gift of faith is simply having the confidence that whatever you're being prompted to do will not fail no matter what. In other words, no matter how impossible the task or how impossible the need may be, you know it is going to come to pass. It's the type of faith that Jesus used in cursing the fig tree in Mark 11:12-14. Jesus didn't sit there and beg and plead and cry out but, instead, with full confidence stated, "Let no one eat fruit from you ever again." Look at the results:

Now in the morning, as they passed by, they saw the fig tree dried up from the roots. And Peter, remembering, said to Him, "Rabbi, look! The fig tree which You cursed has withered away." So, Jesus answered and said to them, "Have faith in God. For assuredly, I say to you, whoever says to this mountain, 'Be removed and be cast into the sea,' and does not doubt in his heart, but believes that those things he says will be done, he will have whatever he says. Therefore, I say to you, whatever things you ask when you pray, believe that you receive them, and you will have them. (Mark 11:20-24 NKJV)

In one 24-hour period the words of Jesus came to pass and the tree was dead, dried up from the roots. When the gift of faith is in operation, there is no demon in hell that can stop what we have declared according to the authority of the Word.

The gifts of healings are healing power of God imparted to those in need. Again, as the spirit wills, this gift will manifest. It is not based on our faith or our ability but as God moves sovereignly in our midst. This is the gift that was in operation when Jesus called forth Lazarus. In the early church we see it in Acts 5 in Peter's ministry.

And believers were increasingly added to the Lord, multitudes of both men and women, so that they brought the sick out into the streets and laid them on beds and couches, that at least the shadow of Peter passing by might fall on some of them. Also, a multitude gathered from the surrounding cities to Jerusalem, bringing sick people and those who were tormented by unclean spirits, and they were all healed. (Acts 5:14-16 NKJV)

This gift was evident in the Apostle Paul's ministry:

Now God worked unusual miracles by the hands of Paul, so that even handkerchiefs or aprons were brought from his body to the sick, and the diseases left them and the evil spirits went out of them. (Acts 19:11-12 NKJV)

The working of miracles constitutes the suspension of the natural process or order of the natural realm. Moses was used mightily in the working of miracles, as seen with the rod tuning into a serpent, the plague of frogs, flies and lice, the locusts, the turning of water to blood and the parting of the Red Sea. We can see Elijah used in this way with the widow of Zarephath when the flour and jar of oil did not run out until the day the famine ended. Other examples that we can look at are Jesus feeding the five thousand, turning the water to wine, and walking on the water.

I was in Haiti in 2001, working in a small church up in the mountains about 60 miles northeast of Port au Prince. We were putting in a new floor in the church while conducting a medical clinic during the day and doing church meetings at night. The church ran the school in the village and part of the enormous mission was feeding the children at the school. The pastor that was hosting us came to me and said, "We have a big, big problem." I asked what the problem was and he told me that they had been told that there were around 150 or so students in the school so that was the amount of food they had bought. The reality was about 250 children in need, not including the workers or our team, of course, that needed to be fed and there simply was not enough food in the natural to go around.

I just began to pray and remind God of what He did with the five loaves and two fishes. I was more than willing to give up my meal so that they could eat but, in the natural, that sacrifice would make a very insignificant difference. By the time they finished serving everyone, not only had the children and teachers eaten, but the people who were from the village helping us and our team also had full bellies. God suspended the natural course of the use of that food and made it enough to feed everyone. In the end, more than 280 people were fed. Whatever the need, God can and will do it. Just obey that which He places in your heart to do so that there are no restrictions on the anointing of God.

8

PRINCIPLES FOR TRAINING OTHERS

In this chapter I want to give some basic principles and ideas for starting where you are as a ministry. It is important that we let God give us creative ideas for winning the lost. I have had the privilege of helping train a church in its first outreach, and over two weekends we went to over 700 homes. We repeatedly went out into the community surrounding the church's location reaching a total of about 1200 homes to offer prayer, witness, and invite the community to special meetings that we held. This resulted in many coming from the community to visit the church. Some stayed, but it definitely created a stir of hunger in those seeking God.

We must be faithful to sow beside all waters, and do whatever it takes to get a congregation mobilized in the community.

"When the Son of Man comes in His glory, and all the holy angels with Him, then He will sit on the throne of His glory. All the nations will be gathered before Him, and He will separate them one from another, as a shepherd divides his sheep from the goats. And He will set the sheep on His right hand, but the goats on the left. Then the King will say to those on His right hand, Come, you blessed of My Father, inherit the kingdom prepared for you from the foundation of the world: for I was hungry and you gave Me food; I was thirsty and you gave Me drink; I was a stranger and you took Me in; I was naked and you clothed Me; I was sick and you visited Me; I was in prison and you came to Me. Then the righteous will answer Him, saying, Lord, when did we see You hungry and feed You, or thirsty and give You drink? When did we see You a stranger and take You in, or naked and clothe You? Or when did we see You sick, or in prison, and come to You? And the King will answer and say to them, "Assuredly, I say to you, inasmuch as you did it to one of the least of these My brethren, you did it to Me. Then He will also say to those on the left hand, Depart from Me, you cursed, into the everlasting fire prepared for the devil and his angels: for I was hungry and you gave Me no food; I was thirsty and you gave Me no drink; I was a stranger and you did not take Me in, naked and you did not clothe Me, sick and in prison and you did not visit Me. Then they also will answer Him, saying, Lord, when did we see You hungry or thirsty or a stranger or naked or sick or in prison, and did not minister to You? Then He will answer them, saying, Assuredly, I say to you, inasmuch as you did not do it to one of the least of these, you did not do it to Me.' And these will go away into everlasting punishment, but the righteous into eternal life. (Matthew 25:31-46 NKJV)

One of the outreach ideas that I would recommend is to visit local businesses and take them a simple bag of candy with a note card to thank them for serving the community. I have done this and the reactions have been broad: from shock, to disbelief, and even some who were near to tears. Imagine if more of the Body of Christ expressed gratitude for the service they receive at a local diner or other establishment in the community. Those who serve in the food or retail industry are often taken advantage of, and unfortunately, some of those taking advantage of them are believers.

ONE PERSON CAN MAKE A DIFFERENCE

Too often we get our eyes on the size of the need for outreach and forget that those around us are individuals, not just masses, not just numbers. I reflect on the story of Abram when his nephew Lot was taken captive. His response was not to focus on the size of the army that had taken Lot, but on the fact that without intervention Lot might be lost forever.

And the king of Sodom, the king of Gomorrah, the king of Admah, the king of Zeboiim, and the king of Bela (that is, Zoar) went out and joined together in battle in the Valley of Siddim against Chedorlaomer king of Elam, Tidal king of nations, Amraphel king of Shinar, and Arioch king of Ellasar—four kings against five. Now the Valley of Siddim was full of asphalt pits; and the kings of Sodom and Gomorrah fled; some fell there, and the remainder fled to the mountains. Then they took all the goods of Sodom and Gomorrah, and all their provisions, and went their way. They also took Lot, Abram's brother's son who dwelt in Sodom, and his goods, and departed. Then one who had escaped came and told Abram the Hebrew, for he dwelt by the terebinth trees of Mamre the Amorite, brother of Eshcol and brother of Aner; and they were allies with Abram. Now when Abram heard that his brother was taken captive, he armed his three hundred and eighteen trained servants who were born in his own house, and went in pursuit as far as Dan. He divided his forces against them by night, and he and his servants attacked them and pursued them as far as Hobah, which is north of Damascus. So, he brought back all the goods, and also brought back his brother Lot and his goods, as well as the women and the people. (Genesis 14:8-16 NKJV)

Abraham was motivated by love for Lot. He was not motivated by personal gain but genuine concern for Lot and his family. Notice that Abram did not wait around for someone else to take care of the need to rescue Lot. He did not say, "Well there is just a few of us. What good would I do?" We must walk in the revelation that the greater One is on the inside of us according to 1 John 4:4. According to Gods word, we can do all things through Christ and we must act on that belief!

CO-LABORING TOGETHER

Being the Body of Christ is not for just one-man! We are here to work and serve together. You can never hire a large enough staff or have enough ministers that could truly meet the needs of a community. The work of the great commission is not for just a select few. God never intended for you to do all the work while everyone else is spoon fed the Word of God.

For we are God's fellow workers; you are God's field, you are God's building. According to the grace of God, which was given to me, as a wise master builder I have laid the foundation, and another builds on it. But let each one take heed how he builds on it. For no other foundation can anyone lay than that which is laid, which is Jesus Christ. Now if anyone builds on this foundation with gold, silver, precious stones, wood, hay, straw, each one's work will become clear; for the Day will declare it, because it will be revealed by fire; and the fire will test each one's work, of what sort it is. If anyone's work which he has built on it endures, he will receive a reward. If anyone's work is

burned, he will suffer loss; but he himself will be saved, yet
so as through fire. (1 Corinthians 3:9-15 NKJV)

When we reach out to the community as a team, we labor
together in God's field, and we build on a firm foundation. We
establish God's work with gold, silver and precious stone. When
we do not authentically care for the body, but build on the hype of
a religious service, we are going to suffer loss. In serving together
as co-laborers, we must give preference to one another. Check
your attitude: We are servants of God; we have given our will to
the will of God.

God has given one senior pastor over a local body that will
lead and direct it as is fitting to Him. Remember, if any of us are
going to be great in God's eyes, we must serve and be a blessing
without a motive of personal gain.

Then He came to Capernaum. And when He was in the
house He asked them, "What was it you disputed among
yourselves on the road?" But they kept silent, for on the
road they had disputed among themselves who would be
the greatest. And He sat down, called the twelve, and said
to them, "If anyone desires to be first, he shall be last of all
and servant of all." (Mark 9:33-35 NKJV)

Don't try to outdo one another, and absolutely don't dominate
the conversations when you are on an outreach or visit. When a
group of two or three people visit or go on an outreach, realize
that God may use any one of you to minister to the need at hand.
Take on the heart of John the Baptist, "He must increase, but I
must decrease." (John 3:30 NKJV) Remember we are stewards of
God and not the owners of His work.

And above all things have fervent love for one another, for
love will cover a multitude of sins. Be hospitable to one
another without grumbling. As each one has received a gift,

Minister it to one another, as good stewards of the manifold grace of God. (1 Peter 4:8-10 NKJV)

Remember that a true servant of God focuses on building and developing others, bringing out the best in them. We must stay focused on coaching and encouraging the gift of God in others, facilitating their growth. When we are interested in listening to the needs of others, God will make sure we have our needs attended to.

When I am ministering to people, I often say very little other than sharing scriptures to the problem they may have. What I have to say is not that important, generally, but if my words truly are of value to another, then God will take care of me. As you are attentive to the needs in their lives, the value you place on people will be recognized.

There is one who scatters, yet increases more; And there is one who withholds more than is right, but it leads to poverty. The generous soul will be made rich, and he who waters will also be watered himself. (Proverbs 11:24-25 NJKV)

Pay attention to the latter part of this verse. When you water others, you are watered by God. He has the greatest accounting system of all time. Think of the time that you sow into others as a seed God can use to bring the harvest of your family and friends into the Kingdom of God.

STAYING FOCUSED

There is always an opportunity to get into a rut. With anything that you do in the ministry I find that what you take for granted you will ultimately lose a passion for. Never lose sight of the fact that we are here to touch as many people as possible. In fact, that's the very reason we are still on the earth and not in heaven.

Don't let yourself get discouraged by the results you can see. Yes, we should see results over time, but when we only are looking for natural manifestations of our work, we are never going to know the full impact of the work and, therefore, lose our drive.

Can you imagine if a farmer who planted seed in the ground and went out after the first day looking for results? Then did the same thing the second and third day and so on? What if he decided he should go dig up the seed and check on it to see if anything was going on? This would not be very healthy for the long-term life of that seed. Depending on the seed, it may take a while to see any growth. For example, an oak tree grows many years before you see the development because it grows down before it grows up. The root structure becomes firmly entrenched in the ground so that when storms come it doesn't just fall over.

God said in Genesis 8:22 that there is seed, time, then harvest. Our problem comes when we don't give the seed the time to grow to harvest. When you go out to minister your perspective and expectations will affect the results. If you go out with the wrong attitude and perspective, you will come back greatly disappointed. Getting and keeping the right perspective will bring the results that honor and glorify God.

Though Jesus knew who would betray Him, He continued to minister. Not everyone you help will do the right thing or even appreciate what you do for them. Always remember, we are serving as unto God, not unto them. Focus on those who are doing the right thing with what you give them. Don't let a small percentage of people become the majority of your focus. Don't lose site of the miracles, breakthroughs and testimonies of lives touched and changed as you go out and let God work through you. We are stewards of God with the message of hope.

And let us not grow weary while doing good, for in due season we shall reap if we do not lose heart.

Therefore, as we have opportunity, let us do good to all, especially to those who are of the household of faith. (Galatians 6:9-10 NKJV)

Walk in the boldness that God gives, being confident of His power being so much greater than anything you will ever face. In 1 John 4:17-18 says, "Love has been perfected among us in this: that we may have boldness in the Day of Judgment, because as He is so are we in this world." The word "perfected" in the Strong's (5048) is teleioo (tel-i-o'-o), meaning to complete, accomplish. As we operate in His boldness we will complete and accomplish His perfect will in the earth.

We can walk with the boldness and confidence in what God has asked us to do when we know that we have His endorsement and His authority to operate with.

ATTENTION TO DETAIL

When you are out visiting with more than 1-2 people, it is important that you decide beforehand who will take the lead. It might seem trivial to say this but always be courteous and always be sincere in your approach to people. Too often, believers come off as insincere or with a 'holier than thou' attitude. I have been with people who were outright rude.

Be well groomed and dress appropriately. Some ministry opportunities may give a little latitude for you to wear jeans or business casual, but you know your culture and community. Setting a standard helps those who need a little more guidance. Be courteous when driving, for example, don't park in driveways or block entrances to neighbor's driveways. If you take too much liberty, you may close the door before you have an opportunity to get through it. Keep your car clean, remembering you represent Jesus, your pastor and your church. Never walk across someone's lawn or through their flowerbeds. If you are invited in and notice everyone's shoes are at the door, take off your shoes. If you respect the rules of that house, the door for ministry will be more open. Simple courtesy goes a long, long way.

When visiting a family, try to eliminate distractions. If the children are disruptive, have one of the team members help keep the children occupied. Use wisdom in this, but it will help you keep the focus on the one you are there ministering to. Be sensitive to any reservations a family may have regarding their children. If the television is on, ask if it is okay to turn off the television. Unless you are invited to stay longer, keep a visit to 15 minutes or less.

I have found it useful to have a door hanger produced with the church information and a note on it with a place for a signature or, as an option, keep note cards with you. If no one is home, there will be something there to let the family know you stopped by. In my experience, just leaving a note alone has done so much to soften the hearts of people who otherwise might have felt they were just a number or that no one genuinely cared.

A SERVANT'S HEART

When you make contact with a person at the home, approach them with the heart of a servant. From the scriptures, the word servant is doulos, which is a slave, an attendant, i.e., wait upon (menially or as a host, friend, to serve. As a servant of God, you are to wholly give your will to the will of another. No minister has a right to be a lord over God's people. He is to be least of all and servant of all. (Mark 9:35 NKJV)

Having your conduct honorable among the Gentiles, that when they speak against you as evildoers, they may, by your good works which they observe, glorify God in the day of visitation. Therefore, submit yourselves to every ordinance of man for the Lord's sake, whether to the king as supreme, or to governors, as to those who are sent by him for the punishment of evildoers and for the praise of those who do good. - - - Honor all people. Love the brotherhood. Fear God. Honor the king. Servants, be submissive to your masters with all fear, not only to the good and gentle, but also to the harsh. For this is commendable, if because of conscience toward God one endures grief, suffering wrongfully. (1 Peter 2:12-19 NKJV)

Never presume that you are so important. Remember, we serve Him and not our own desires and not to gain advantage over others. James 4:10 (NKJV) says, "Humble yourselves in the sight of the Lord, and He will lift you up."

You younger men, follow the leadership of those who are older. And all of you serve each other with humble spirits, for God gives special blessings to those who are humble, but sets himself against those who are proud. If you will humble yourselves under the mighty hand of God, in his good time he will lift you up." (1 Peter 5:5-6 TLB)

As servants of God, we are here to find and meet needs. Think about the Apostle Paul's ministry. He traveled around identifying the needs of churches and those whom he had led to the Lord. He made sure he gave them the tools they needed to be victorious in life.

I urge you, brethren—you know the household of Stephanas, that it is the firstfruits of Achaia, and that they have devoted themselves to the ministry of the saints— that you also submit to such, and to everyone who works and labors with us. I am glad about the coming of Stephanas, Fortunatus, and Achaicus, for what was lacking on your part they supplied. For they refreshed my spirit and yours. Therefore, acknowledge such men. The churches of Asia greet you. Aquila and Priscilla greet you heartily in the Lord, with the church that is in their house. (1 Corinthians 16:15-19 NKJV)

"Yet I consider it necessary to send to you Epaphroditus, my brother, fellow worker, and fellow soldier, but your messenger and the one who ministered to my need; since he was longing for you all, and was distressed because you had heard that he was sick. For indeed he was sick almost unto death; but God had mercy on him and not only on him but on me also, lest I should have sorrow upon sorrow. Therefore, I sent him the more eagerly, that when you see him again you may rejoice, and that I may be less sorrowful. Receive him therefore in the Lord with all gladness, and hold such men in esteem; because for the work of Christ he came close to death, not regarding his life, to supply what was lacking in your service toward me." (Philippians 2:25-30 NKJV)

Our focus is serving others—don't be distracted or a distraction to those we serve or those who lead us. Proverbs 28:20 (NKJV), "A faithful man will abound with blessing."

THE IMPORTANCE OF PRAYER

Prayer and fasting are important keys to outreach, visitation and any ministry in the local church. Find out which members of the church are willing to reach out to, pray for and witness to others. Specifically, find out, who they'll be contacting and follow-up with them for progress reports and accountability. Always place an emphasis on seasons of fasting and prayer for the lost.

And when they had come to the multitude, a man came to Him, kneeling down to Him and saying, Lord, have mercy on my son, for he is an epileptic and suffers severely; for he often falls into the fire and often into the water. So, I brought him to Your disciples, but they could

*not cure him. Then Jesus answered and said, "O faithless
and perverse generation, how long shall I be with you?
How long shall I bear with you? Bring him here to Me.
And Jesus rebuked the demon, and it came out of him;
and the child was cured from that very hour. Then the
disciples came to Jesus privately and said, why could we
not cast it out?" So, Jesus said to them, Because of your
unbelief; for assuredly, I say to you, if you have faith as
a mustard seed, you will say to this mountain, move
from here to there,' and it will move; and nothing will
be impossible for you. However, this kind does not go out
except by prayer and fasting. (Matthew 17:14-21 NKJV)*

Remember that without faith we will never please God. So
when we pray for the lost or pray for people when we are out,
we must do it in faith. As you minister to people, praying in the
Spirit will help you keep your focus and hear what God wants to
do for each person you connect with.

*Likewise, the Spirit also helps in our weaknesses. For we
do not know what we should pray for as we ought, but the
Spirit Himself makes intercession for us* [a] *with groanings
which cannot be uttered. Now He who searches the hearts
knows what the mind of the Spirit is, because He makes
intercession for the saints according to the will of God.
(Romans 8:26-27 NKJV)*

You can also pray prayer of agreement before and after a
visit. Placing a strong emphasis on prayer will keep people from
getting in strife and will keep peace in your outreach ministries.

9

KNOWING WHO YOU HAVE

As stewards of the time and ministry that God has given us, it is vital we know exactly who are the members, regular attendees, and potential attendees of our church.

For which of you, intending to build a tower, does not sit down first and count the cost, whether he has enough to finish it— lest, after he has laid the foundation, and is not able to finish, all who see it begin to mock him, saying, 'This man began to build and was not able to finish.' Or what king, going to make war against another king, does not sit down first and consider whether he is able with ten thousand to meet him who comes against him with twenty thousand? (Luke 14:28-31 NKJV)

Prioritizing visits I have listed below some guidelines I use when considering who to visit and who to call. If someone has been completely unresponsive to contacts after a 90-days, consider moving them to an inactive file. Send them quarterly updates or when special events are planned. If you only focus on those who are unresponsive, you will have no time for the current and new members of your congregation.

1-WEEK ABSENTEES:

Print out a call list for the pastor or lay leader to express care and offer prayer. Make note of any prayer requests or needs, and notify the appropriate ministry. If they express an interest in serving, get their name to the appropriate ministry leader. The more proactive you are in overseeing your flock, the fewer opportunities the enemy has to bring havoc to their lives.

2-WEEK ABSENTEES:

Export a list of members and regular attendees who have been out for two weeks. Create a spreadsheet of the city (I.E.: north, south, or zip code lists) and sort the spreadsheet in zip code order. Once the list has been reviewed/edited, map the addresses in an app. If you have more than one team or person visiting the members of your church, divide the list into groupings of 10-12 addresses. Thanks to the continued advance of technology, a spreadsheet in zip code order will usually help keep you in a smaller area, allowing you to make the most of your time.

3-WEEK ABSENTEES:

Export a list of members and regular attendees who have been out for three weeks. Again, create a spreadsheet of the city (north, south, etc.) and sort the list in zip code order. Once the list has been reviewed proceed to the mapping program. Divide the list into a grouping for a pastoral or lay minister visit. The quicker we reach out to these members, the more likely we will be able to help them with the issue(s) that have kept them away.

ACTIVE MEMBERS AND REGULAR ATTENDEES

When I was first assigned this task many years ago, I needed to get a full understanding of who we had in the church. I visited the entire church in a 30-day period roughly 300 visits. It is very important that your current members and regular attendees feel that there is a system of care to pull on in a time of need. Please hear my heart, I am not encouraging you to create an environment that allows people to stay in the infancy of their faith. However, a personal touch builds confidence in people. The more consistent we are in building relationships, with and in the body, the more strength we have as a body. No matter where you are if you focus and organize your team you can visit anywhere from 50-100 homes in a week by making short and simple visits. With the innovation of new technology for mapping and church contact management, it is possible to do this without having a staff of hundreds. As you develop leaders who can work with you in this ministry, you will be able to spend more time focusing on the ones who may need more in-depth ministry.

NEW CONVERTS AND VISITORS

To visit it is of the utmost importance that in addition to visiting the people who have been missing. Additionally, there must be an emphasis placed on the new converts and visitors to your church. Make an effort to contact the new convert and visitor within the first 24-48 hours after their conversion or first visit to your church. This first contact can be a call from the care team, but don't let it stop there. If they have given their lives to Christ recently, make sure a leader and, possibly, the person who brought them stop by their home. Giving them personal attention will continue to fan the flame of their faith.

God has a very special place in His heart for the new convert. We are responsible as a body to make every effort to not allow the seed that has been sown into the hearts of people to be stolen by the enemy.

"Go therefore and make disciples of all the nations, baptizing them in the name of the Father, and of the Son and of the Holy Spirit, teaching them to observe all things that I have commanded you and lo I am with you always even to the end of the age." (Matthew 28:19-20 NKJV)

If you do not have a system of follow-up in place, how will you truly make disciples? If having a New Convert class were enough, then we would have much higher retention rates. We must get out of the four walls of the church so we can assimilate people into the Body of Christ. Listed below are the steps I use and have been effective for follow-up.

1. On Sunday afternoon, make phone contact with them by having a leader or minister from the staff call to let them know you are praying for them and that you are there to serve them if a need arises.

2. Take the time to visit them within 24-48 hours and encourage them to attend a class that next Sunday structured just for them or if you do not have classes such as Sunday School or New Believers, offer to meet with them for coffee or something.

3. Send them a letter on Monday, from the Senior Pastor, congratulating them on their decision in the altar call.

4. If you have small groups, have a group leader call them around mid-week. Invite them to the group or some other church event, mid-week service, etc. It is most effective if you have the small group leader in their area or a leader with like interest contact them.

5. Have a minister or church leader call again by Friday or Saturday of that week. Remind them of services on Sunday and offer help in meeting any counseling or other needs that may have been found on the initial visit.

PRIORITIZING VISITS

Everyone in the church is important. But if you do not make a list of priorities, you will lose momentum quickly. Categorize visits and put them in order of importance, this will allow you to maximize your time. If your ministry is stable and there are no current challenges, you should strongly emphasize new converts and visitors. This will continue to bring new life to your church and encourage and challenge the church family to reach more people.

This kind of approach is like having a new baby in the house--only on an eternal scale. When you see new believers and new families being added to the church and the fruit remaining from your efforts, everyone will be blessed.

10

CONCLUSION

The first step to getting the church excited about discipleship is to get an understanding of why many churches are in the shape they are today. I have been through the same challenges everyone faces who answers the call to the ministry. I have also learned from my own failures and those of others which principles in life must be followed. God intends for all of us to have a fruitful and productive life and ministry as a part of the Body of Christ.

John 15:8, states that God is glorified when we bear much fruit and so we will be His disciples indeed. The only way to bear the "much fruit" is to abide in Him, fulfilling His commandment of love. His agape love will motivate us to action to see the lost, the prodigal and disconnected people grow deep roots so they can grow up.

Studies from groups like The Barna Group and The Billy Graham Evangelistic Association to name a few have shown that a key factor to whether a church grows or declines is how they handle the follow-up with visitors and inquiries of that local body. The congregation must first desire growth. According to church growth experts congregations that participate in inviting new attendees and visitors are 63% more likely to grow than those that do not. These congregations are more likely to create a sense of belonging, a place of spiritual growth and vitality. Since their focus is not inward, like a social club, the environment is that of a close-knit family.

While programs and events may gather masses, what is done after they have come into a congregation is the key that determines the effectiveness of the program or event. The most basic aspect to growing a congregation is follow-up. The more thorough and persistent the follow-up, the greater the retention and growth. Making calls, sending letters, and conducting personal visits all factor in to productive follow up.

I firmly believe that we must be persistent and assertive with the follow-up of the first-time visitor to our churches. Herb Miller's book, "How to Build a Magnetic Church" says that when lay members make a 15-minute follow up visit to the home of a first-time visitor within 36 hours, the return of those people is as high as 85 percent. I have personally experienced the result Herb Miller speaks of in the churches I have led and been part of.

Additionally, I believe it is important to think outside the box and get creative. For example, a young person showing up at their house is not as effective as showing up at a ball game. I have done this and, does it make a impact. This type of approach allows you to get to know them as well as develop a relationship with them. They see the sincerity of your heart and the love of God in a practical way.

My strength in the ministry has been that of the personal contact. To do this we must create an environment of discipleship in our ministries. Look at the model the Book of Acts has laid out for us. That pattern shows personal discipleship in the word, fellowship, breaking of bread, and prayer will make a dramatic difference in the growth of the church. Growth isn't about numbers for the sake of numbers; it's about true disciples. As Isaiah says, "For precept must be upon precept, precept upon precept, Line upon line, line upon line, Here a little, there a little. (Isaiah 28:10 NKJV)

God's pursuit of man has been fervent from the fall until now. No matter what sin man has found himself in, God has always found one who would walk before Him preserving the He could use to bring us a Savior. Noah, being a man who would respond to God, saved himself and his family, and was given the assignment to, "Be fruitful and multiply and fill the earth." (Genesis 9:1 NKJV)

Through that bloodline came the Patriarch Abraham. He was given the covenant that his decedents would be as the "stars of the sky in number." (Genesis 15:5 NKJV) This promise would not come through the son he had with his wife's servant, but only through Sarah. With God nothing is impossible. Though Sarah was 90 years old and Abraham 99, God made what impossible with man, possible because Abraham believed that God was able.

God's plan, however, was never designed for one person to do it all. Not even Jesus did everything Himself when he was on the earth. He showed His disciples the heart of God. He selected the twelve, whom He later named Apostles. The pattern Jesus modeled for us should be seen in our ministries today. There must be those that we raise to another level of ministry and care for the Body of Christ.

After training the twelve, Jesus sent them out. Then He sent out seventy others. Through His ministry, we can see the principle of multiplication and increase. Many ministers make a fatal mistake by thinking they must do all the work or that five-fold ministers are the only one's "anointed" to reach people. The Apostle Paul penned these words to the church at Ephesus.

> *And He Himself appointed some to be Apostles, some to be Prophets, some to be evangelists, some to be pastors and teachers, in order fully to equip His people for the work of serving—for the building up of Christ's body— till we all of us arrive at oneness in faith and in the knowledge of the Son of God, and at mature manhood and the stature of full-grown men in Christ. So, we shall no longer be babes nor shall we resemble mariners tossed on the waves and carried about with every changing wind of doctrine according to men's cleverness and unscrupulous cunning, making use of every shifting device to mislead. But we shall lovingly hold to the truth, and shall in all respects grow up into union with Him who is our Head, even Christ. Dependent on Him, the whole body—its various parts closely fitting and firmly adhering to one another—grows by the aid of every contributory link, with power proportioned to the need of each individual part, so as to build itself up in a spirit of love. (Ephesians 4:11-16, New Testament in Modern Speech)*

Whether it's a letter, call, or visit, much more must happen with follow-up than to passing the visitor information card to a secretary for input into a database. There must be an active, concerted effort in the local church to reach out to those who come through our doors. We must develop teams of people to be out and on the doorsteps of our visitors every week.

> *...But God composed the body, having given greater honor to that part which lacks it, [25] that there should be no schism*

in the body, but that the members should have the same care for one another. (1 Corinthians 12:24-25 NKJV)

When the Body of Christ is equipped through the local church, each part working in the function and capacity God has given and anointed. We will see many more reached for the Kingdom of God.

The book of Acts should be our template for increasing and multiplying those who are being saved and added to the church. When we train, equip, and disciple the Body of Christ, we will present to Him a glorious church without spot or wrinkle, and our assignment will be complete. When the day of accounting for our stewardship comes, we will hear, "Well done good and faithful servant, you were faithful in a little thing; be ruler of a great thing and enter into the joy of your Lord." (Matthew 25:21 NKJV)

In closing, I want to encourage you with a ministry tool I created called, "The Mandate: Discipleship Training Workbook." It is designed to be a tool in the hand of the believer to help them personally make disciples. Written in outline form, it will help you walk a new believer, into a strong foundation in their walk with Jesus step by step. It can be used in a classroom setting, small group, or over a longer period of time if that fits your ministry best.

May you be blessed in all you set your hand to, and may we see the Body of Christ greatly multiply in these last of the last days!

Made in the USA
Middletown, DE
25 October 2023

41340202R00084